WORLD OF CULTURE

DANCE

by Jack Anderson

Newsweek Books, New York

NEWSWEEK BOOKS

Joseph L. Gardner, Editor

Janet Czarnetzki, Art Director
Edwin D. Bayrd, Jr., Associate Editor
Laurie Platt Winfrey, Picture Editor
Kathleen Berger, Copy Editor
Ellen Kavier, Writer-Researcher
Mary Ann Joulwan, Designer

S. Arthur Dembner, President

ARNOLDO MONDADORI EDITORE

Giuliana Nannicini, Editor

Mariella De Battisti, Picture Researcher
Marisa Melis, Editorial Secretary
Enrico Segré, Designer
Giovanni Adamoli, Production Coordinator

Contents

1

Bodies in Motion

So MUCH OF OUR UNIVERSE is in motion. In outer space, planets circle the sun. Our own circling planet, the earth, turns upon its axis—a pattern of motion that is repeated within each atom, where spinning electrons circle a nucleus of protons and neutrons. In this cosmos of perpetual motion, our own bodies naturally and instinctively react to situations through movement before we verbalize a response. We shrink with fear, throw up our hands in surprise, or reach out to embrace someone we love. Looking around us, we behold the stately passage of the seasons and the inexorable passage of each separate life from birth to maturity to old age and death. Life itself is movement.

No wonder, then, that one of the oldest of the arts is the art of movement—dance. Assuming one form or another, it flourishes everywhere. Its origins are rooted in the prehistoric past, for long before dance grew to be a complex art early man took pleasure in swaying, turning, stepping, and stamping rhythmically, just as small children do today. Aware of the movement of the powerful forces of nature, early man moved in ways he hoped would appease those forces or give him power over them. Hunters danced before pursuing their quarry, warriors danced before battle, tribes danced to exorcise evil spirits and to propitiate the gods. There were dances to bring rain, dances to celebrate the harvest, dances of birth, puberty, marriage, and death.

Each of the world's great civilizations has produced its own dances. In one sense, all have been similar, since all have made use of the body in motion. But because the body can move in so many ways, dance forms have varied enormously from culture to culture. Those of Asia are the most complex, in part because Eastern dance, like Eastern art in general, is intimately associated with religion and is, therefore, contemplative in character. This is particularly true of certain styles of Indian dance, an outgrowth of the fact that Hindus believe that the world was created by a dancing god, Lord Shiva. The dances developed in India make use of intricate gestures involving not only the arms but such parts of the body often slighted in the West as the ankles, neck, nose, wrists, and eyes.

Over the centuries a number of Asian nations have blended dance with other arts to attain a composite theatrical form. Two of the major styles of traditional Japanese theater—the fastidious Noh and the more robust Kabuki—combine dance with recitation and singing. And native

For more than a thousand years ritual dances have been a part of everyday life on the island of Bali. In the ketjak, *or monkey dance (seen opposite), villagers gather before a burning lamp to conjure up the spirit of the monkey who, according to the ancient poem* Ramayana, *helped the Hindu god Rama free his wife from captivity.*

Chinese theater makes no clear-cut distinction between dance, drama, opera, juggling, and acrobatics.

The ancient Greeks saw, in the formal order of dance, an instance of mind and body in perfect harmony—and as a result dancing occurred at religious festivals as well as at weddings and funerals. The choruses in Greek plays are said to have danced while they chanted, although comparatively little is known about how these performers actually moved. Tragedies contained dignified dances, while there were vigorous and sometimes lewd dances in the comedies.

Although scorned by early Christian moralists, dance could not be uprooted. In Western culture, dance exists both in such international manifestations as the classical ballet and in purely regional traditions. A much admired instance of the latter is the flamenco dance of Spain, famous for its fiery stamping and heel patterns.

Wherever dancing prospers and whatever bodily movements different cultures favor, there are at least two basic kinds of dance. One exists primarily for the benefit, edification, or amusement of the dancers who perform it. Folk and ballroom dances are examples of this form, which is based on the presumption that dances such as the waltz may be fun to look at but are even more fun to take part in. The other

The graceful movement of the body through space and time is a facet of dance that transcends both historical eras and national customs—as can be seen in the Greek statuette shown above, the sixteenth-century Indian ivory carving at left, and the nineteenth-century ballerina depicted in the drawing at lower right.

basic kind of dance assumes that its movements can be watched with pleasure; in fact, it exists to be watched. This kind of dance might be called theatrical dance, and it includes such otherwise disparate manifestations as ballet, modern dance, Japanese Noh, and the choric passages in Greek tragedy.

But dance is not the only kind of movement people enjoy watching. There is the pleasure of watching fire in the grate, waves on the beach, raindrops on the windowpane, and passersby in the street. Baseball and football have been called spectator sports, and certain graceful movements in fencing and basketball have even been compared to dancing. Several factors distinguish dance from these phenomena. Unlike sports, dance is not—or at least should not be—a competitive activity. The excitement of sports arises not only from how the game is played but from a desire to know who will eventually win the game. The excitement of dance arises solely from the event itself. Should a ballet be well performed, then, in a sense, all its dancers win. Theatrical dance usually involves far more complex emotions than do sports, and it is certainly more structured than the flickering of fire or the jostling of pedestrians.

Dance is movement that has been organized so that it is rewarding to behold, and the craft of making and arranging dances is called choreography. Out of all the possible movement combinations that exist, the choreographer selects, edits, heightens, and sharpens those he thinks are suitable for his specific purposes. The gestures in some dances may refer to specific emotional states and their sequence may tell a story. Other dances tell no story, but instead present beautiful images of people in motion, the choreographer believing that pure movement in itself is worthy of attention. Because dance can assume so many guises, the viewer should regard each dance he attends with fresh, unprejudiced eyes. All dance styles are not alike, and some, to the uninitiated, may look decidedly odd.

Usually dances are accompanied by suitable music, but while a score may do much to emphasize a work's rhythmic vitality or to establish its emotional atmosphere, music and dance are not invariably linked. Some dances are set to sound effects or to literary recitations; others are performed in silence. Similarly, scenery and costumes may contribute to a work's effectiveness, but some worthy dances require nothing more than simple tunics and a bare stage.

However quirky or individualistic a specific work may be, the fundamental appeal of all theatrical dance is that of seeing everchanging shapes. Dancers inhabit space and time simultaneously, and the interest of a dance derives from the space they use and the time they take, from the positions of their bodies, from their energy, dynamics, and the way their steps are rhythmically organized into units of effort and rest. Dancers may cover great territory or huddle in a corner. They may run, leap, turn, dart, glide, or amble; their movements may seem light or heavy, large or small, taut or slack, quick or languid.

From all this activity and interactivity the dance is built. Whether it tells a story, preaches a message, or conjures a mood, dance communicates because it prompts responses within us. Dance is not simply a visual art, it is kinesthetic as well; it appeals to our inherent sense of motion. As we watch dancers onstage, our own muscular systems react to the strain or relaxation of their movements. We not only observe what happens, we also, in some empathic way, feel it.

The art of dance is as old as the human race, but specific dance forms are much younger. And viewed in relation to the traditions of the Orient, the genres most common in Europe and America, the ones usually referred to as ballet and modern dance, are comparative newcomers. They were conceived only a few centuries ago, but their short history is an extraordinarily eventful one.

2

The Dancing Kings

THE YEAR WAS 1581, the place was Paris, and the occasion was the marriage of Marguerite of Lorraine, sister of Queen Louise, to the duc de Joyeuse. In theory, the prospective bride's brother-in-law, King Henri III, was the nation's dominant political figure, but in actuality all matters of state were deeply influenced by the king's mother, Catherine de Médicis, who had left her native Italy years before as the bride of the duke who eventually became Henri II. A wily, self-indulgent autocrat, Catherine wanted the forthcoming marriage to be a magnificent occasion. She therefore sought assistance from one of her valets, a fellow Italian who was named Baldassarino de Belgiojoso but who was known in France as Beaujoyeulx.

Drawing upon his training as a musician and dancing master, Beaujoyeulx devised an entertainment that fully matched the queen mother's expectations. This *Ballet Comique de la Reine*, staged in the Salle Bourbon of the Louvre Palace on October 15, 1581, was the most important early attempt at creating an extended choreographic spectacle. It was undeniably a spectacle, but it only vaguely resembled anything we would now term ballet. For one thing, there was no stage; the action took place on the floor of the hall itself. Most of the audience sat in galleries along three walls, while the royal family sat on a dais at one end of the room. Although its title contained the word *comique*, the production was not humorous; in this instance *comique* was derived from *comédie*, the French word for drama. And although it was called a *ballet*, the program contained songs and recitations as well as dances. Collectively they tell of how the enchantress Circe conquers nature with her sorceries and makes herself queen of the seasons. In the end, the Greek gods defeat her and Athena pays tribute to a far greater queen—the queen of France. Louise, the object of this tribute, actually participated in the production, appearing in one interlude on a float adorned with sirens and tritons that spouted water as it moved across the hall. At the conclusion of the ballet—which lasted nearly six hours—symbolic medals were exchanged, Queen Louise giving her husband the king a signet emblazoned with a dolphin. Since the royal couple did not have a son—and since the French word *dauphin* can refer both to the sea creature and to an heir apparent—the medal's Latin inscription, *Delphinum ut delphinem rependat*, was a matrimonial pun: "A dolphin is given to receive a dauphin."

The tradition of entertaining visiting dignitaries with elaborate spectacles featuring music, poetry readings, mime, and dance began in Renaissance Italy but soon became familiar at the French court as well. As the sixteenth-century view at left suggests, it was customary for the royal couple themselves (center) to lead the dance.

The *Ballet Comique* must have pleased Catherine, for she distributed illustrated accounts of it around Europe. Beaujoyeulx's opus was indisputably a pioneering work, but it could hardly be called totally original. Indeed, it could fairly be said that Europe had always danced. Even during the sternly repressive decades of the Middle Ages, when clergymen associated the soul with goodness and the body with sin, dance had persisted in street fairs and courtly ceremonies. A favorite subject of medieval artists was the dance of death, which featured a skeletal figure who led people of every social estate in a dance that suggested the grim democracy of the grave. This dance was only depicted, yet equally strange dances were actually performed during the Middle Ages. Weird outbreaks of dance mania were said to have occurred in the midst of sacred services, for instance, and there are reports of the craze possessing whole congregations.

In castles and palaces across Europe, dances served as party entertainments—this despite the fact than one such spectacle, the *Bal des Ardents* of 1393, nearly claimed the life of Charles VI, king of France. On that particular occasion, Charles and several of his retainers had elected to dance before the court disguised as savages, chained to each other and wearing bizarre costumes covered with tow and pitch. Apparently their makeup was so convincing that no one present could tell who the players were, and when the duke of Orléans bent forward for a closer look, the torch he was carrying set fire to the dancers' costumes. Charles, who had decided only moments before that he would rather chat with the duchess of Berry than perform and who had therefore slipped his chains, escaped immolation when the duchess threw the train of her dress over him. The other dancers died in agony, however, save for one gentleman who managed to douse himself with water.

Court dancing—of a more civilized and choreographed sort—was to flourish throughout the Renaissance, particularly close to the source of that great cultural rebirth. At the time, Italy was not a unified nation but rather a collection of squabbling states ruled by princes adept at intrigue. These princes desired nothing so much as to increase their prestige and impress their neighbors, and one way to do so was to encourage art and learning and create a brilliant court. Ostentatious by nature, dance was especially well-suited to such needs, and it quickly became popular. As a result, it was in Italy that the first dancing masters appeared, among them Domenico of Piacenza, who in about 1400 wrote the earliest surviving European treatise on dance. He and his followers, Antonio Cornazano and William the Jew, were everywhere in demand to create dances for state occasions. The very word "ballet" is Italian in origin, derived from the verb *ballare*, "to dance."

Italian dance productions were often extremely lavish. A particularly curious example of the genre is the dinner ballet that Bergonzio di Botto produced in 1489 at a banquet celebrating the marriage of the duke of Milan. Vaguely akin to a modern nightclub floor show, it consisted of several loosely related scenes, each based upon classical mythology and each pertaining to the dinner course that it accompanied. Jason's Argonauts captured the Golden Fleece—and the guests ate roast lamb; Diana went hunting—and the diners fell upon a stag.

The engraving at right portrays the opening scene of Beaujoyeulx's Ballet Comique de la Reine, *the earliest presentation in which music, drama, and dance were combined. Although it cost in excess of three million francs, the* Ballet Comique *delighted its patron, Catherine de Médicis, mother of the weak French king Henri III. Elegance of dress and carriage were hallmarks of the members of Henri's entourage (above) who participated in court balls.*

12

Whether lavish or simple, these spectacles would have to be termed amateur theatricals, for they were presented by nobles rather than by professional dancers. Moreover, ballet steps scarcely differed from those of the ballroom, there being as yet no essential difference between social and theatrical dance. The latter was simply more polished and more studied.

Significantly, the ballroom form itself was already quite polished by the 1500's, for the dancing master was also expected to set standards of

Dance entertainments sometimes struck an exotic note. In the Bal des Ardents *(left), King Charles VI of France and his retainers dressed as beastlike savages in costumes that proved highly flammable. An accident during the performance resulted in the immolation of all save Charles and one other dancer. During the sixteenth and seventeenth centuries, equestrian tattoos (below) provided a diverting change from traditional stage dramas.*

etiquette and deportment. This linking of art and manners is the subject of a charming dance manual of 1588 called *Orchésographie*. Written by Thoinot Arbeau, the pseudonym of a benign, worldly French priest, it contains a series of dialogues between Arbeau and a young pupil in which several popular dances, military marching, flute and drum playing, seemly behavior with the ladies, and proper grooming are all discussed at some length.

In Arbeau's time, dancing—like riding or fencing—was considered a gentlemanly accomplishment. Sometimes these skills overlapped, as when, for example, it was discovered that horses could learn to dance. The horse ballet, which enjoyed a certain popularity from the sixteenth century onward, consisted of horses dancing in complicated formations, their trainers thereby combining the functions of riding master and dancing master. The horse ballet survives today in what is known as haute école riding, and among the foremost attractions of modern Vienna are the white Lippizaner stallions of the Spanish Riding School. Superbly trained horses dance with great refinement in an elegant exhibition hall that was built in 1729.

Of far greater consequence are the sixteenth- and seventeenth-century dances for humans, many of which are still known to us. These

include the courtly pavane and the galliard, a vigorous dance, full of leaps and kicking steps, that usually followed the pavane. Other dances were the swift courante, which featured running and gliding; the lavolta, in which a young lady, assisted by her partner, leaped and turned in midair; and the stately sarabande, which was occasionally forbidden because moralists thought it lascivious. Considerable finesse was required in executing these dances, but there was comparatively little virtuosity involved—and most of the virtuoso steps that did exist were assigned to men. Similarly, although women performed ballroom dances, female roles in the balletic spectacles were customarily played by men or adolescent boys.

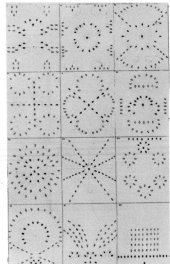

Like the *Ballet Comique de la Reine*, many productions were designed for halls in which some members of the audience sat above the action. This led to an emphasis upon geometrical floor patterns, with dancers forming and reforming squares, diamonds, ovals, and triangles. The age delighted in allegory, and some of the figures thus formed came to have symbolical meanings. An account of 1610 states that the triangle symbolized Justice, three circles conjoined meant Truth Known, a square within a square was Virtuous Design, and three circles within one another stood for Perfect Truth. Dancers could also form letters of the alphabet or words. Thus, for example, in *Salmacida Spolia*, an English masque of 1640, nymphs spelled out "Anna Regina," referring to Anne of Denmark, mother of Charles I. The skeptical English essayist Francis Bacon chided that "turning dances into figures is a childish curiosity," and many sobersided adults would doubtless agree. Still, it is clear that the child in us ever welcomes these curiosities—witness such comparable modern phenomena as football half-time drills and the chorus routines of Busby Berkeley movies.

By the end of the sixteenth century dancing was in vogue at every court in Europe. England's Queen Elizabeth loved to dance, and it is said that every morning, as a setting-up exercise, she leaped through six or seven galliards in succession. Spectacles involving dancing were popular in England from the time of Henry VIII, but they attained their most elaborate form in the seventeenth-century Jacobean masques writ-

In seventeenth-century Florence dance emphasized the grandeur of mass movement, either on foot or on horseback. Equestrian ballets such as the one at left, presented in honor of the prince of Urbino, were organizational triumphs that followed strict geometrical plans (below, left). In other cases, ballrooms were turned into vast stages (right) where spectators could easily shift from merely viewing to actually performing.

Overleaf: Ballets à entrée, popular at the court of Louis XIII, often featured parodies of the dress and manners displayed by those who attended the king.

17

Entrée Des Esperducattis

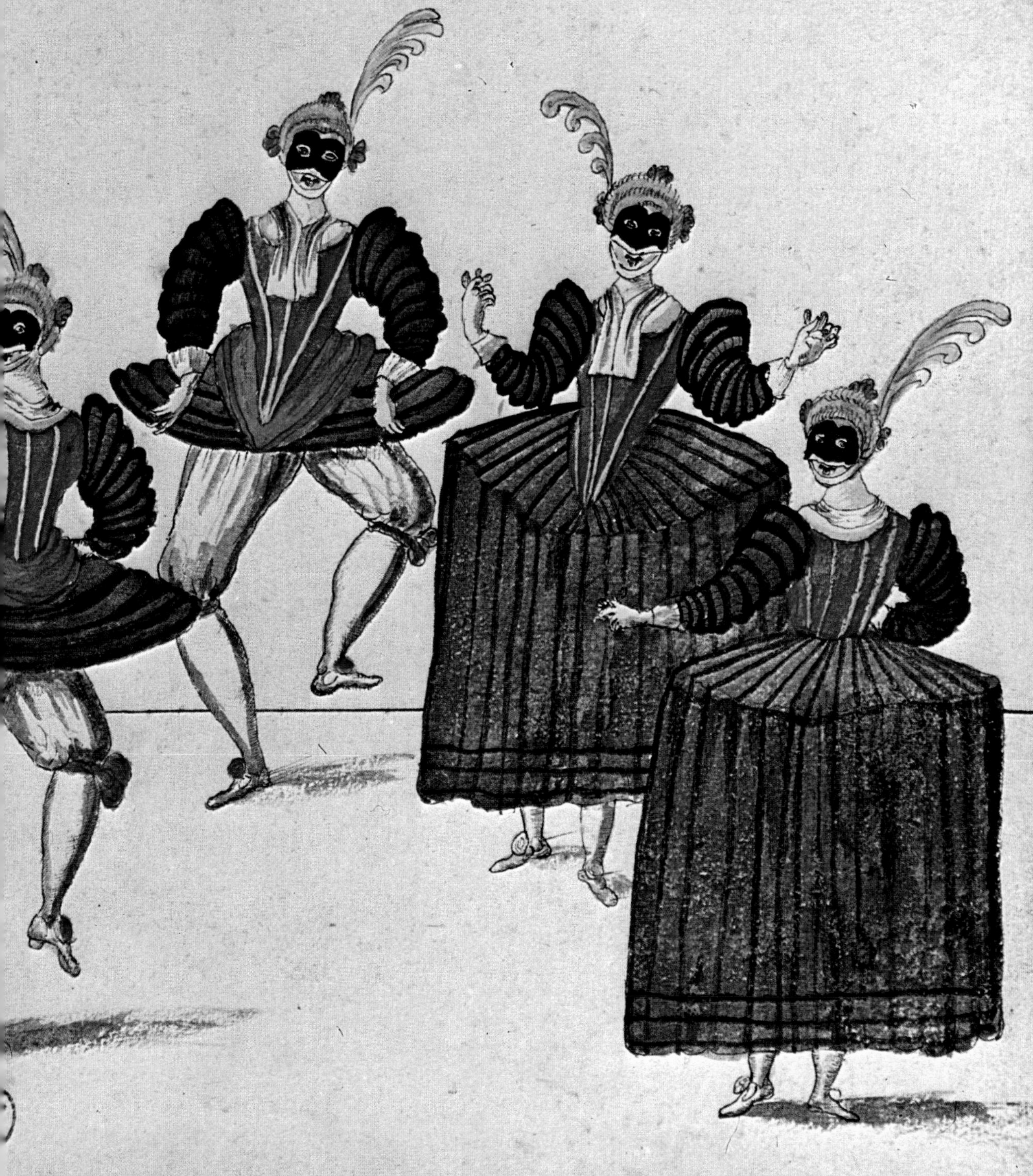

ten by Ben Jonson and designed by Inigo Jones. Interestingly enough, because these masques stressed literary over choreographic elements, they have ultimately proved more important to the history of drama than to the history of ballet.

In France the popularity of ballet was a manifestation of French interest in Italian culture. By this time French court life had become excessively refined and stratified, and every social encounter had become as intricate as choreography. Dance naturally prospered in such a milieu, and consequently balletic carriage and manner are aristocratic in nature and ballet steps retain French names. Even today, ballet at its most stylish remains an art whose skilled practitioners possess the airs and graces of a French aristocrat. They are part of the aristocracy of

dance, but they have attained their place through talent and work rather than mere accident of birth.

Louis XIII himself appeared in French court ballets, for which he occasionally wrote both the scenario and music. Although he was often cast in suitably dignified roles—as the spirit of fire that cleanses impurities and destroys enemies, for example—he is said to have preferred comic parts and to have enjoyed portraying women. A popular form of entertainment in Louis' time was the *ballet à entrée*, a series of independent scenes, ranging from the solemn to the grotesque, that were linked only by a broad general theme. The flexibility of this type of

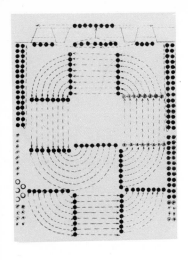

Many of the steps and costumes used in the seventeenth-century dance pageants were only exaggerated versions of real-life manners and dress. The four gentlemen at left, performing in a ballet à entrée, were undoubtedly courtiers themselves. The large numbers of people and animals involved in early ballets required the director to set each dance carefully, as the neatly drawn diagram above shows.

episodic construction made possible works ranging from the simple and economical to the lavish and costly. The grotesque scenes often called for performers far nimbler than even the most skilled courtiers—and it was for this reason that professional entertainers began to be hired after 1630. And as the demands on dancers grew more rigorous, the number of professionals employed increased.

The first decades of the seventeenth century were to bring other significant changes to balletic form. The most important of these was that ballet moved from ballrooms and halls into proscenium theaters. There most members of the audience could face the dancers straight on—a change that permitted choreographers to emphasize individual human figures as well as massed ensembles. This factor further hastened the professionalization of dance. In its own subtle fashion, the proscenium theater stressed ballet as something to be seen by others, whereas previously it had been witnessed and performed by the same people. In effect, the proscenium created a psychological gulf between participant and viewer. At first that gulf was not wide, however, for early proscenium theaters had ramps extending from the stage to the auditorium floor to permit performers and spectators to dance together at the end of the ballet, and until well into the eighteenth century members of the audience were allowed to sit on the stage.

French court ballet reached its creative apogee under Louis XIV, whose remarkable reign spanned the years from 1643 to 1715. Louis, who first danced in public in 1651 at the age of thirteen, took ballet quite seriously. Indeed, it was in a ballet that he was first introduced as the living embodiment of the Sun King. Louis had in fact been associated with the sun throughout his life, a medal struck at his birth having proclaimed him *Orbis Solis Gallici* ("The Risen Sun of Gaul"). In 1653 he portrayed the Rising Sun in the *Ballet de la Nuit*, a symbolic representation of the times of day. During its penultimate episode, thieves under the cloak of night attempt to loot a burning house, but at the conclusion Aurora enters accompanied by the Rising Sun, Honor, Grace, Love, Riches, Victory, Fame, and Peace. This allegory was neither as simple nor as harmless as it now sounds, for only two years before a mob had actually dared to invade the Palais Royal to protest high taxes and poor living conditions. Since then, dissent had been quelled. France was not to become a burning house; the Rising Sun, the absolute monarch, was to reign triumphant, enthroned in virtue. The audience at *Ballet de la Nuit* had been given much to ponder.

The self-proclaimed incarnation of *gloire*, Louis made his entire existence a theatrical spectacle. By means of royal visits and processions, he lived in full view of his subjects, who were, after all, his audience. The course of Louis's day was as regular as the sun, as measured as a dance. Art and life were virtually one and the same for the king and for his court, and under the circumstances it is little wonder that ballet was so admired. In its formality, ballet must have seemed the apotheosis of the social structure, the triumph of order. Since the dancers were courtiers, in dancing they could become living myths and, offstage, could perpetuate mythology by modeling themselves upon such balletic characters as Apollo or Alexander the Great. Court life had become a matter of perpetual artifice, and personality had become a matter of sustained impersonation.

Louis chose talented artists to produce his ballets: the poet Isaac de Benserade provided scenarios; Jean Bérain designed opulent scenery and costumes. Many of the costumes were inspired by the heroic styles of the Roman Empire, but the historical research involved in creating them was slight and the results suggested a fantastical antiquity rather than any actual period. Certainly no Roman ever wore a *tonnelet*, the wide and cumbersome hooped skirt of mid-thigh length that became the standard costume for male dancers and continued to be used into the eighteenth century.

Many court ballets were composed by Jean Baptiste Lully, who came to France as a boy from his native Florence, where he had been a comic dancer. In Florence, he had also grown familiar with the semi-improvised antics of the commedia dell'arte. This robust entertainment, with its stock characters such as Arlecchino and Pulcinella, profoundly

influenced French ballet and theater, particularly French comedy. Lully, who possessed such comic talent that he could make Louis XIV weep with laughter, danced in some thirty ballets, but his greatest contribution was as a composer of gracious, sophisticated music. A ruthless schemer in private life, he managed to dominate French musical activities until his death in 1687.

Theatrical productions of this period were frequently hybrids: operas contained dancing, ballets contained recitations and songs. If dance still was not recognized as an autonomous art, the mixing of the arts nevertheless led to works of great sumptuousness. It also made possible a lighthearted mode, the *comédie-ballet*, developed by Lully and the great comic playwright Molière. Consisting of spoken scenes inter-

Louis XIV was an active and an ardent admirer of the dance throughout his lifetime. Before advancing age and sheer portliness put an end to his career, the French king often performed in the ballets composed by Jean Baptiste Lully. At right, Louis appears in the costume of Apollo, the Greek god of the sun and patron of the arts. The scenarios of many early ballets were published in elegantly decorated editions, of which Filippo d'Aglié's Il Gridelino (left), first performed in Turin, Italy in 1653, is a notable example.

Apollon. ~~~~~~~~~~~~ *Le Roy.*

spersed with danced interludes, this theatrical form might be considered a distant ancestor of the musical comedy. One of the best examples of the genre, *Le Bourgeois Gentilhomme*, continues to amuse audiences to this day. Molière's story of gullible, middle-class Monsieur Jourdain —who, in his desire to ape the aristocracy, takes singing and dancing lessons and is finally fooled into believing that he has been made an Oriental potentate—offers considerable opportunities for clowning. At its premiere in 1670, Lully, who had written the score, also played the role of the Mufti.

The leading dancing master of the time was Pierre Beauchamps, Louis XIV's teacher. His ballets, like those of many illustrious old choreographers, have been forgotten for generations. But from prints and writings it is possible to assess and analyze the techniques he employed. Balletic fundamentals were beginning to be stressed, including the five fundamental foot positions, which had been recognized at least since 1700. And to quote Lincoln Kirstein, director of the New York City Ballet, these positions were to come to constitute "a kind of net or comb through which dance movement must accommodate itself in its ceaseless shift."

Beauchamps would probably gasp with astonishment at a modern ballet, for contemporary ballet dancers bring to movement and position a mastery of the principle known as turn-out (meaning that professional ballet dancers are capable of turning their legs outward from the hips at a 180-degree angle). In Louis XIV's day, when dancers wore high-heeled shoes and bulky costumes, turn-out was minimal. Over the centuries, however, ballet masters have discovered that turn-out helps the dancer increase his flexibility and balance while simultaneously permitting the body to open outward and face the audience in its maximum silhouette, thereby facilitating clarity and visibility of movement. Thus turn-out has become a cardinal principle of ballet—although individual choreographers, of course, retain the liberty to abolish it in order to produce unusual special effects.

Professionalism in dance increased after 1670, when Louis XIV stopped appearing in ballets. Perhaps he had noted the lines in Racine's *Britannicus* that criticized a monarch for flaunting himself in public. Racine was referring to Nero, but Louis apparently appreciated the parallel. In any event, the young king, although only in his thirties, was growing noticeably stout. Louis still enjoyed ballet, of course, and he was so eager for the art to survive that long before he retired he took pains to insure that this would happen. Among other things, he established in 1661 the Académie Royale de Danse, an association of teachers who were given a meeting room in the Louvre but who preferred to convene at a nearby inn. Nothing much came of this organization and it eventually disbanded, but its founding indicated that official recognition was being given to dancing. In 1669 Louis took a more important step: he founded the Académie Royale de Musique, which exists today as the Paris Opéra. As dancers appeared in its productions from the beginning, the Paris Opéra Ballet can boast of being the world's oldest ballet company. The Académie's first production, the opera *Pomone*, was given in 1671 in a converted tennis court. Managerial

The Paris Opéra has provided a home for ballet for over three centuries. Among the innovations premiered on the Opéra stage was the first appearance by professional female dancers—in Lully's Le Triomphe de l'Amour *(right). Prevailing fashions determined the degree of movement a dancer could exhibit, as contemporary sketches (above) of two Opéra performers indicate. Mlle des Chars, seen at top, was hindered by the cumbersome gown she wore, while M. Balon's much shorter tonnelet allowed him to perform with comparative lightness and ease.*

quarrels almost caused the venture to collapse, but Lully intervened,
reorganized the academy, and wielded power there for years.

Louis's retirement as a dancer and the opening of the Opéra hastened
the downfall of the court ballet and accelerated the growth of totally
professional ballet. This dance form was to be an art for both sexes,
with women as well as men trained to appear on the Opéra stage. Thus
it was that in 1681 a Mlle Lafontaine led three other ladies in Lully's
Le Triomphe de l'Amour. Since all were soloists, they might all be
called ballerinas; and since Mlle Lafontaine was their leader, she might
fairly be called a prima ballerina—the first in history. Little else is
known about her, but her very presence was a sign that the noble amateur, the dancing courtier, was about to bid the stage adieu.

3

The Birth of Ballet

Had Catherine de Medicis lived to attend the Paris Opéra during the early eighteenth century, she would unquestionably have been taken aback by what she saw. Yet the splendor of the ballets performed there would not have been totally alien to that strong-minded lady, nor would their form have been incomprehensible. True, the proscenium theater had replaced the galleried hall, and professional dancers had replaced the courtiers of Catherine's day, but rigid distinctions were not yet being made between social and theatrical dances. The most popular ballroom dance of the period, the minuet, was also performed in ballets—and wherever it was danced, on stages or in salons, it employed balletic steps and made use of turn-out and the five positions of the feet.

An opera fan of the early 1700's might well have boasted that a new form, the *opéra-ballet*, had come into existence. This form was related to the old *ballet à entrée*, however, since it consisted of independent scenes linked by a common theme and utilized both singing and dancing. The technical resources of the proscenium theater encouraged the use of spectacular stage effects, and *opéra-ballet* attained its dramatic apotheosis in the compositions of Jean Philippe Rameau, whose *Les Indes Galantes*—complete with dancing flowers and an erupting volcano—enjoyed immense popularity, both when it was first staged in Paris in 1735 and when it was revived there in the 1950's. Could she have seen it, Catherine de Médicis might have sighed, "Ah, if only Beaujoyeulx could have worked on such a stage!"

While many productions, despite their fancy new trappings, were really descendants of the old court ballet, genuinely fresh ways of creating ballets were also being explored, and the eighteenth century witnessed the rise of both the star dancer and the innovative choreographer. Professionalization encouraged dexterity, and the opening of the Paris Opéra Ballet School in 1713 insured a steady supply of dancers. One Opéra dancer, Louis Dupré, was called "*le grand Dupré*" because of his imposing presence and "the god of the dance" because of his majestic movements. He danced until he was sixty, his stateliness increasing yearly.

Among Dupré's pupils was Gaetan Vestris, a member of a dancing family that dominated the Paris Opéra for more than half a century, from the days of Mme de Pompadour through the Revolution and into

A man of consummate grace and elegance, Gaetan Vestris dominated the Paris Opéra in the latter half of the eighteenth century as a dancer, teacher, and choreographer. The multitalented Florentine is shown opposite in costume for the ballet Plaisir. *Vestris' most famous pupil was his son Auguste, who succeeded his father as the greatest male dancer of his era.*

Napoleonic times. Like his teacher, Gaetan was nicknamed "god of the dance," and Dupré seems to have bequeathed his favorite pupil both his arrogance and his noble style. Gaetan passed on this vanity to his son Auguste Vestris. In one respect, though, Auguste differed from his father: instead of specializing in majestic poses, he was a virtuoso noted for turns and jumps. Like some of his predecessors, he continued to appear when he was past his prime, then retired to become a distinguished teacher.

Two ballerinas—Marie Anne de Cupis de Camargo and Marie Sallé —were particularly admired. They constitute an instructive pair for the historian, since they personify rival artistic viewpoints that remain in opposition even today. Both dancers were pupils of the ballerina Françoise Prévost. Otherwise, they were utterly dissimilar, onstage and off. Camargo was worldly, the toast of Paris; Sallé, in contrast, was quiet, reserved, an apparent model of propriety. She was also the leading dramatic dancer of her day, and although she appeared successfully in Paris, London was the scene of many of her greatest triumphs. There she staged the dance accompaniments for Handel operas, and in so

Over the years, interest in ballet has been whetted by the fortuitous juxtaposition of individuals possessing great talent but strikingly different artistic outlooks. The first great rivalry of this nature sprang up between Marie Camargo and Marie Sallé in the early 1700's. Camargo, shown in the engraving at left, became an outstanding technical virtuoso, while Sallé, seen in the portrait at right, brought a new degree of expressiveness and characterization to the dance.

doing became one of history's first female choreographers. Her most revolutionary accomplishment was to choreograph a ballet version of the Pygmalion fable in 1734, in which she played the sculptor's statue, magically come to life. On this occasion, Sallé discarded the cumbersome costumes of the day, particularly the wig and the *panier*, a hooped petticoat that was the female equivalent of the male *tonnelet*. Instead she wore a simple muslin dress and shoes without heels. Her natural hair, without a jewel or ornament, fell loosely to her shoulders. People fought in the streets to see her at Covent Garden.

Camargo was different altogether. She was a virtuoso acclaimed for her grace and verve, qualities which became apparent so early that Prévost, fearful of losing her supremacy, had Camargo relegated to the last row of the Opéra's ensemble. Then one night, when a male dancer missed his entrance, Camargo leaped forward and completed his solo with aplomb. Thereafter, success followed success for her. Voltaire remarked that Camargo was the first ballerina to dance like a man. By this he meant that she was the first woman to acquire the technical

P.Rameau Invenit et fecit.   ex. cum privilegio Regis.

brilliance theretofore associated with male dancers. In her time she was celebrated for her *entrechat*, a flashing step in which the dancer crosses his legs repeatedly while in the air. Today, in a more complex form, the *entrechat* remains a step beloved by male virtuosos. So that audiences could see her version of the step, Camargo shortened her skirt.

Camargo's costume reforms differed from Sallé's, however, for they were prompted by quite distinct considerations. Camargo wanted her accomplishments to be seen without hindrance, whereas Sallé wanted to portray a specific character. Camargo and Sallé have thus come, perhaps inevitably, to symbolize two approaches to the art of dance, the former representing dance as beauty of outward form, and the latter representing dance as the expression of inner urgency. Interestingly enough, similarly convenient pairings occur in other periods of dance history. There are, for example, the ethereal Taglioni and the passionate Elssler in the nineteenth century, and the classical Pavlova and the impassioned Karsavina early in our own century. Both approaches can be valid, of course, for taste often swings from one ideal to another. Thus, when the Camargo dancer's formal perfection suddenly seems academically correct but dull—or simply degenerates into empty acrobatics—there tends to be new interest in the Sallé dancer's expressive power. But should the Sallé dancer offer self-indulgent melodrama, the virtues of the Camargo dancer are again extolled.

Succeeding Camargo and Sallé in the affections of Parisians was Barberina Campanini, called La Barberina. Trained in Italy, where the schools emphasized speed and prowess (as they would for more than a century to come), Barberina amazed audiences with her turns and *entrechats*. Barberina's offstage life was as lively as her dancing. In Berlin, Frederick the Great installed her as his mistress. He dined with her, had her portrait painted, and applauded her with gusto. And that, perhaps, was all he did, for Frederick's affections did not tend toward the opposite sex and Barberina was his mistress in name only—her presence balancing a circle of intimates that was otherwise completely male, thereby forestalling any scandal. For her part, Barberina carried on with many other young men throughout the period of her liaison with Frederick. Curiously enough, she was to end her days as the abbess of a convent, dying there in 1799 at the age of seventy-eight.

Barberina's progress from theater to nunnery is by no means atypical of the period. It also suggests the moral ambivalence with which dancers were regarded. On the one hand, the Church officially condemned the theater and would neither marry nor bury actors or danc-

ers. Yet on the other, bishops and cardinals would hire dancers to entertain at their banquets, and a few even took dancers as their mistresses. It was assumed as a matter of course that female dancers would have affluent men as lovers, and it comes as no surprise that many of these women, born of poor families, welcomed the gifts—the jewels, the gold, the fine food and wines—their admirers lavished upon them.

Condemned by contemporary moralists, dancers were nevertheless indispensable to the pleasures of respectable society. No wonder many were shrewd and devil-may-care, living loose lives when young and officially repenting in old age. Under such circumstances, their improprieties sometimes seem a burst of hearty paganism surviving both the

The two dancers portrayed in the engraving at left are engaged in intricate maneuvers mapped out by an unknown choreographer. They are looking down at their feet in an effort to master the floorplan of the dance. At right is one of the lavishly costumed dancers who appeared in Jean Philippe Rameau's tragic opera-ballet Hippolyte et Aricie.

threats of hellfire and the frowns of hypocrites. Occasionally, this paganism was lusty indeed. Some dancers appeared in pornographic shows at private theaters attended by courtiers, intellectuals, and clerics in disguise. One such theater was on the estate of Marie Madeleine Guimard, a ballerina celebrated for her dramatic stage presence, her flamboyant love life, her general extravagance, and her charity to the poor.

Just as dancers extended ballet technique, choreographers developed new dance forms. The most important of them was the *ballet d'action*, which, unlike the sprawling *ballet à entrée*, sought narrative coherence. Several experiments in this mode were made early in the eighteenth century, one sponsored by the duchess of Maine, who was an intellectual, a wit, a dwarf, and an insomniac. Intellect and insomnia conspired to induce her to present nighttime entertainments at her château.

There, on one occasion, dancers from the Opéra mimed an act of Corneille's *Horace* that had been set to music. Although successful, the experiment was regarded more as an eccentric lady's latest curiosity than as a fruitful way of making ballets. More ambitious was *The Loves of Mars and Venus*, staged in London in 1717 by John Weaver, with Dupré as Mars. This is thought to be the earliest complete ballet to convey dramatic action through movement, obviating speech and song. It had little immediate impact, but in manner it sounds vaguely akin to Sallé's *Pygmalion*, produced seventeen years later, and consequently some historians believe that Sallé saw Weaver's choreographic work during her youth.

Midcentury found the *ballet d'action* thriving. Its popularity helped ballet separate itself from opera and drama and attain artistic independence. Through this liberation the choreographer gained a creative power that he had not enjoyed in court ballets and *opéra-ballets*, where he was often only one member of a team dominated by a playwright or operatic composer. Still, one should avoid the glib assumption that everything before the *ballet d'action* was somehow inferior. If the *ballet d'action* encouraged unity, the *ballet à entrée* encouraged variety and contrast; and if the *ballet d'action* emphasized drama, the *ballet à entrée* emphasized display. Here is yet another instance of how balletic taste can swing between concern for movement purely for its own sake and concern for movement as a vehicle for emotional expression.

The principal advocates of the *ballet d'action* were Gasparo Angiolini and Jean Georges Noverre. Personal enemies in their own day, they have become artistic allies through historical perspective. A pupil of Franz Hilverding, a Viennese pioneer of the *ballet d'action*, Angiolini collaborated with Christoph Gluck, staging the Elysian Fields scenes in the opera *Orfeo ed Euridice* and creating the ballet *Don Juan*, which possesses possibly the best score of any eighteenth-century choreographic work. The story of Don Juan's philandering and eventual damnation rushes along in accordance with Angiolini's belief that ballets should not be encumbered by subplots. Nothing survives of his 1761 choreography, but the ballet's taut scenario has inspired many choreographers to do their own versions of *Don Juan*.

Noverre first won acclaim in 1754 when he choreographed *Les Fêtes Chinoises*, a ballet on Chinese themes, at the Paris Opéra Comique. Chinoiserie was the rage at the time, and Noverre's ballet was so exotic that the English actor David Garrick invited him to produce it at Drury Lane in London the following year. The invitation was ill-timed, for England and France were on the verge of the Seven Years' War and anti-French sentiment was high. Though Garrick spread the rumor that Noverre was really Swiss—he was, in fact, half Swiss—his ballet occasioned rioting and its run was curtailed.

A traveler about Europe, Noverre amused Frederick the Great with comic impersonations of ballerinas, traded spicy stories with Voltaire, and headed a large, fine company in Stuttgart. In Vienna he gave dancing lessons to the young Marie Antoinette and, like Angiolini, he worked with Gluck. He walked into a rehearsal of *Alceste* one day and saw Gluck throw his wig to the ground in rage because he could not

Like many innovators in the arts, Jean Georges Noverre (above) expended the better part of his talent and energy in a struggle against the reactionary forces he sought to supplant. It was through the offices of Marie Antoinette, pictured below, that Noverre finally achieved a major goal—appointment as ballet master at the Paris Opéra. Many of Noverre's ideas finally came into prominence as a result of the work of such students as Jean Dauberval, seen at upper right in the ballet Tancredi.

Overleaf: In the eighteenth century the ballet was still an entertainment of the upper class, although its setting had shifted from the ballroom to the theater. This change of venue is indicated in miniature on the cover of a period snuffbox.

get his chorus to move expressively. Noverre suggested placing the singers in the wings while dancers mimed to the music—an expedient that proved enormously effective.

Noverre occupies a pivotal position in dance history because of his *Letters on Dancing and Ballets*, published in 1760. In this dance manifesto he argued that ballets should be unified works of art in which every element contributes to the development of the main theme, that technical exhibitions for their own sake should be discouraged, and that such impediments to movement and expression as heeled shoes and cumbersome skirts should be abolished. These proposals are relevant not only to the *ballet d'action* but to modern ballet as well, and they help to explain Noverre's considerable influence upon the course of dance history. Noverre put his theories into practice in several works, including *Jason and Medea* (1763), which made such an impact that a 1780 account called it a "*Ballet Terrible*, ornamented by dancing, suspicion, darkness, pleasure, horror, gaiety, treason, pleasantry, poison, tobacco, dagger, *salade*, love, death, assassination, and fireworks."

Some of Noverre's ballets were considered fine examples of psychological realism when given their premieres. Yet concepts of natural and expressive action vary across the centuries, and consequently what Noverre's audiences thought realistic may now seem florid. Moreover, Noverre did not always achieve the aims he set forth in his *Letters*. He could not persuade all dancers to adopt costume reforms, for example, and while *Jason and Medea* caused some spectators to faint, less overwrought viewers insisted that Noverre's choreography contained too much stately parading about. Worst of all, perhaps, was the fact that Mozart, who composed *Les Petits Riens* for him, pronounced Noverre deficient in musicality.

Happily, Noverre was to live to see many of his proposed costume reforms adopted. In the three decades following the French Revolution, costumes approached Noverre's ideals of "light and flowing draperies," and the heeled dancing shoe gave way to the heelless slipper. Indeed, not until Isadora Duncan adopted Greek robes in our own century would dancers go so scantily clad. Corsets and fancy costumes

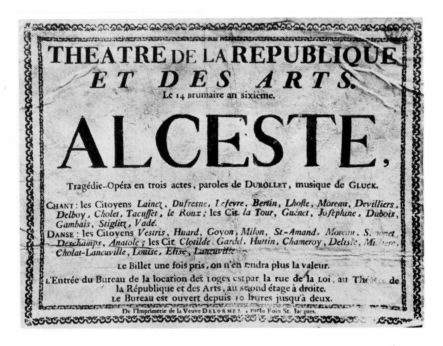

Possessing remarkably similar artistic outlooks, Noverre and composer C.W. Gluck on occasion collaborated with memorable results. The Gluck opera Alceste, for example, was premiered in an Italian version in Vienna and a French version in Paris. The poster at left, above, announces an Opéra production in which Gaetan Vestris—whom Noverre considered the most perfect artist of the period—led the dancers. At right, a dancer imaginatively costumed to portray one of the four elements in an eighteenth-century ballet d'action.

returned in the nineteenth century, but the *tonnelet* and *panier* were abolished forever.

By the time of the Revolution ballet was attracting a wider public, and choreographers, looking beyond classical mythology, started borrowing themes from ordinary country life. Their rustic ballets were often as fundamentally unrealistic as the little dairy farm that Marie Antoinette commissioned so that she might play at being a milkmaid. Yet their existence was a sign of changing tastes.

Not a scrap, not a step remains of the works of Noverre or Angiolini. But in 1786, a pupil of Angiolini's named Vincenzo Galeotti staged *The Whims of Cupid and the Ballet Master* in Copenhagen for the Royal Danish Ballet—and the Danes, miraculously, have preserved it ever since. Some of the steps are currently danced with embellishments that would not have been possible in 1786, but by and large it seems a reasonable example of eighteenth-century choreography. This oldest extant ballet, which shows Cupid mischievously mixing up pairs of lovers from several countries, happens to be genuinely amusing—much to the relief of the dance historian, who, forced by necessity to take so many reputations on faith, can at last breathe easily when he discovers that a ballet considered jolly by its first audiences proves to be jolly when produced today.

One other comic work of the period also survives, after a fashion. It is *La Fille Mal Gardée*, produced in Bordeaux in 1789 by Jean Dauberval, a choreographer famous as a womanizer and as a creator of witty and sweetly sentimental ballets. The inspiration for *Fille* came when Dauberval passed a shop window and spied a print showing an old woman throwing a hat after a youth fleeing from a cottage where a peasant lass was seen weeping. From this print Dauberval developed his story of two young lovers who frustrate the best efforts of the girl's scheming mother to marry her off to a wealthy simpleton. Dauberval's choreography has been lost, but choreographers continue to be charmed by his sunny, tender scenario. The ballet lived on in Russia throughout the nineteenth century under the title of *Vain Precautions*. More recently, the American Ballet Theatre has produced a version based upon Russian sources, while Frederick Ashton has choreographed an entirely new version for England's Royal Ballet that many critics consider among the comic masterpieces of twentieth-century dance.

During the late eighteenth and early nineteenth centuries, possibly as a result of the influence of early Romantic writers and such artists as Jacques Louis David, Jean Auguste Dominique Ingres, and Bertel Thorvaldsen, heroic ballets were very much in vogue. The master of this genre was the Italian choreographer Salvatore Viganò, who also happened to be the nephew of the composer Luigi Boccherini. Viganò dared on a grand scale; his ballets include *Richard Cœur de Lion*, *Joan of Arc*, *Othello*, and *Coriolanus*. Several factors distinguished these works, which Viganò termed *choreodrammi*, from the mythological works common during the early days of the *ballet d'action*. One was fervor and scale; they were big, exultant affairs. Second, instead of alternating mime and dance, as many choreographers did, Viganò combined them in continually unfolding dramatic movement. Statuesque poses and groupings, often based upon classical sculpture, were contrasted with sweeping ensembles.

As a result, Viganò's opponents accused him of relying too heavily on mime and not enough on real dancing. This kind of charge, raised against dramatic ballets in many periods, is worth examining. Sometimes it is justified, as when a ballet consists largely of frantic gesticulation. But there are other times when those who complain that a dramatic ballet contains too little dancing are merely revealing that their personal taste inclines toward decorative or abstract, rather than dramatic, movement. In recent years, of course, experimental choreographers have called into question the whole distinction between dance and nondance movements, and in this light some of the implications of both Viganò's practice and the arguments against it seem unexpectedly contemporary. So, too, are the implications of Viganò's use of music. Although Beethoven composed *Prometheus* for him, most of Viganò's scores—like those of other choreographers of the period—were medleys taken from various composers, music being tailored to the dance in a manner resembling the way musical potpourris were assembled to fit the action of such silent films as *Birth of a Nation*. Here again there is opportunity for debate. Some theorists would find Viganò musically weak, while others—those for whom movement alone is the paramount ingredient of dance production—might claim him as a forerunner of those early modern dancers who deliberately kept their accompaniments rhythmically functional and spare so that they would not possess interest independent of their use in the dance. Whatever the strengths and weaknesses of his ballets may have been, Viganò had ardent admirers, among them the novelist Stendhal, who confidently pronounced him "the Shakespeare of the dance," an honorific title that Garrick had earlier bestowed upon Noverre.

Dramatic expression was also among the aims of Charles Didelot, who staged works throughout Europe, most notably in St. Petersburg, where he exerted a profound influence upon Russian ballet. Like Viganò, he sought dramatic clarity and often modeled group scenes upon paintings or sculpture. He, too, was championed by a great writer —the poet Pushkin claimed that there was more poetry in Didelot's ballets than in all French literature of the time. (Didelot reciprocated by basing a ballet upon Pushkin's *The Prisoner of the Caucasus*.) Didelot was also interested in stagecraft. He placed mirrors onstage so that the spectator could behold the same dancer from several angles, and he promoted the use of tights, thereby contributing to the simplification of costuming. Most spectacularly, for his *Zephyr and Flora* of 1796, he devised a system whereby dancers could be lifted into the air on wires, giving the illusion of flight. The effect was sensational and was much imitated; sylphs were soon flitting across the stages of Europe.

But something even more innovative also happened, for by means of wires, Didelot could lower a ballerina to the floor in such a way that she seemed poised on the tips of her toes. Soon—very soon—ballerinas would know how to balance on their toes without being held by wires. But the mastery of that secret belongs to a whole new era of ballet.

The ballets Dedalo *by Salvatore Viganò (below) and* Zephyr and Flora *by Charles Didelot (opposite) both reflected the trend toward a more cogent realization of dramatic themes that dance manifested in the early part of the nineteenth century.*

ZEFFIRO E FLORA

4

Moonbeams and Gossamer

FROM THE STAGE MANAGER's point of view, the Paris Opéra premiere of Giacomo Meyerbeer's *Robert le Diable* in 1831 was an unqualified disaster. The leading tenor accidentally tumbled through a trapdoor, and another singer was nearly hit by a falling gaslight. A dance episode began with the ballerina poised on a tomb. Fortunately, the choreography required her to gaze upward—where what she saw was no heavenly vision but a piece of scenery that had torn loose from the flies and was hurtling toward her. She jumped to safety in the nick of time. Despite these calamities, *Robert le Diable* was a critical and popular success. In part this was due to the fact that it contained a ballet sequence so novel as to be almost unprecedented. This episode was set in a ruined cloister, where the ghosts of lapsed nuns emerged from their tombs to dance by moonlight. Shifting moonbeams—an effect created by suspended gas jets—played over the Gothic ruins and dancing spectres, and they caused audiences to shiver deliciously. It did not matter that some critics found Filippo Taglioni's choreography confused in design; the overall mood was unforgettable, as was the unearthly presence of the choreographer's daughter, the ballerina Marie Taglioni, who seemed not to dance but to float. Nothing quite like this had ever been seen before, and it marked the first balletic triumph of the artistic movement known as Romanticism.

The Romantic era in ballet extends from about 1830 to 1870 and reflects parallel tendencies in all the arts and in society. It was, among other things, a time of profound social upheaval. Radical ideas were being voiced, but memories of the excesses of the French Revolution and of Napoleon's defeat afforded reminders that fervor could go astray. At the same time, a new wealthy class—a middle class grown rich through commerce and industry—was achieving prominence. This class, which discovered opera and ballet and patronized theaters, brought with it a wave of materialism, prudishness, and hypocrisy. Only a few years before the premiere of *Robert le Diable*, for example, all *danseuses* at the Opéra had been commanded to lower their skirts so as not to inflame the male spectators.

Rebelling against smugness and obsolete forms, young artists celebrated feeling and passion. The poems of Lord Byron and Victor Hugo, the paintings of Eugène Delacroix, and the music of Hector Berlioz and Franz Liszt—all reflected a desire to experience life at fever

The lavishly appointed Paris Opéra was the scene of the 1831 premiere performance of Meyerbeer's opera Robert le Diable, *a success attributable in large part to the spectacular choreographic effects devised by Filippo Taglioni and performed by his daughter, Marie, in the famous "Dance of the Nuns."*

pitch. Two aspects of Romantic art—a concern for the colorful things of this world and a hankering after the nonrational and supernatural—united in Romantic ballet. Inspired by Spain, Italy, or Egypt, choreographers filled ballets with touches of local color and episodes from folklore. (It has also been suggested that the Industrial Revolution may have had something to do with this interest in foreign locales. For it is certainly true that while improved transportation made it easier to visit strange places, industrialism simultaneously threatened their unspoiled charm.) Combining realism with escapism, Romantic ballet afforded entertainment that was part travelogue, part fantasy, and part nostalgia.

Much Romantic art is characterized by a sense of yearning, by a bittersweet awareness of the gulf that exists between aspiration and actuality. The twentieth-century choreographer George Balanchine has said, "To be Romantic about something is to see what you are and to wish for something entirely different. This," he adds, "requires magic." Choreographers sought magic in the fancies of legend and in a tendency to emphasize the emotional and intuitive, rather than the rational aspects of human nature. Ballets about elves and naiads became popular. So did ballets about madness, sleepwalking, and opium dreams. As a result, certain works of this period give the sociologist or psychologist much to ponder. Take Filippo Taglioni's *The Revolt in the Harem*. It depicts harem wives, aided by the Spirit of Womankind disguised as a slave, rebelling against their oppressors—making it possibly the first ballet about the emancipation of women. Equally curious items are *Gemma*, a ballet about an evil hypnotist's attempts to seduce a girl through mesmeric suggestions, and *La Volière*, the story of an older woman, unlucky in love, who tries to raise her younger sister in total ignorance of the male sex. When at last a man does appear, she tells the girl he is a kind of bird and must be caged. Interestingly enough, both works were choreographed by women.

After 1822, theatrical sorcery became easier to conjure, thanks to the increasingly widespread use of gas-lighting, which permitted flickering contrasts of brightness and gloom appropriate to nocturnal or supernatural landscapes. Designers quickly took advantage of these illusions, which collectively necessitated a major change in stage design. Before 1829 the Paris Opéra never lowered the curtain between scenes of an opera or ballet. By lowering the curtain—as audiences discovered when Giacchino Antonio Rossini's *William Tell* was staged in this new fashion —scenic surprises could be prepared and unveiled. At about this same time it also became customary to lower the houselights during performances, and the darkened auditorium and trembling gaslight helped make the theater a place of wonders.

Robert le Diable's cloister scene hinted at the possibilities of choreographic Romanticism; *La Sylphide*, in 1832, explored them on a grand scale in a two-act ballet. Choreographed by Filippo Taglioni for his daughter, the latter ballet featured music by the composer Jean Madeleine Schneitzhoeffer. *La Sylphide* tells of a spirit of the air, a sylph, who falls in love with a young Scotsman on the day he is to be married. Torn between the real and the ideal, he deserts his human fiancée to run off with the sylph. A witch gives him a scarf and, unaware that

The ethereal beauty of Marie Taglioni (above) typified the sublime and otherwordly spirit that was a hallmark of the Romantic movement in ballet. In the nineteenth-century engraving at right of a scene from Filippo Taglioni's La Sylphide, *the distraught hero, James, tries in vain to catch the elusive sylph.*

it is enchanted, he ties it around the sylph's waist. As soon as he does so, her wings fall off and she dies. This story of love between a man and a spirit is typically Romantic, and Filippo Taglioni combined the two aspects of balletic Romanticism—the earthy and the fantastical—by filling the first act with Scottish dances and the last with lighter-than-air dances for the sylph and her attendant sprites. Thematically, *La Sylphide* poignantly expresses Romantic yearning for the unattainable and shows that as soon as anything sought for is grasped, its character changes.

La Sylphide gave Marie Taglioni the finest role of her career. She was so convincing a sylph that droves of other dancers tried to emulate her, thereby initiating a tendency toward the idealization—and idolization—of women in ballet. Taglioni's illusion of airy femininity was enhanced by her costume, which had a tight bodice and a bell-shaped skirt that reached almost to the ankle. Unlike the light draperies of the previous era, the so-called Romantic tutu concealed the dancer's figure in masses of billowing material, leaving only the ballerina's bare neck and shoulders to hint at flesh-and-blood reality. Though dancers later shortened their costumes, it was the Romantic tutu that succeeded in associating ballerinas with supernatural visions.

Filippo Taglioni's choreography was forgotten generations ago, but *La Sylphide* survives in a version as authentically Romantic as the origi-

nal. In 1836, in Copenhagen, August Bournonville, desiring to display the talented young Lucile Grahn, choreographed his own *Sylphide* to new music by Hermann von Lovenskjold. This version survives in the repertoire of the Royal Danish Ballet and other companies.

Born in Copenhagen, where his father directed the Royal Danish Ballet, August Bournonville received advanced training in Paris in Auguste Vestris' classes and subsequently appeared at the Paris Opéra. He returned to Copenhagen in 1830, and, with sporadic interruptions, spent most of his life there as dancer, teacher, choreographer, and company director. Grahn herself is said to have indirectly caused one interruption, which occurred in 1841. Some years before, in a contractual dispute, she had been dismissed. Her admirers kept demanding her reinstatement, however, and they therefore hissed Bournonville, the company's director and leading male dancer, during the middle of a performance. Angered, Bournonville turned toward the royal box and asked King Christian VIII, "What is Your Majesty's command?" "Go on," said the king. Bournonville continued the performance—and the next day the king banished him for six months. By involving the monarch in a petty squabble Bournonville had offended Christian's dignity and was therefore guilty of *lèse-majesté*. The exile proved a fruitful one, however, for Bournonville visited Italy, where he gathered material for some of his brightest creations.

Thanks to the way the Danes have preserved them, the extant Bournonville ballets constitute the only surviving body of works by any Romantic choreographer. Some, like *La Sylphide* and *A Folk Tale*, which is based upon Scandinavian legends, reflect the Romantic interest in the supernatural, while others derive from the customs of such regions as Italy (*Napoli*), Flanders (*The Kermesse in Bruges*), and Denmark's own provinces (*The Volunteer Guards on Amager*). Still others are topical: *Far from Denmark* was inspired by a Danish vessel's voyage around the world, while in *Konservatoriet* Bournonville offers an affectionate portrait of ballet classes in the days of Vestris.

Bournonville's choreography favors swift and delicate footwork, intricate beats, and the springiness ballet teachers call *ballon*. Some of these qualities may stem from Bournonville's attempts to hide his own personal defects. He had a brittle way of landing his jumps and he tried to disguise this by inventing sequences in which the landing is followed not by a sustained pose—which would permit spectators to scrutinize him for faults—but by an immediate take-off into another movement. The resultant Bournonville style emphasizes elevation and strength in its steps for men, sweetness and charm in its steps for women. Among contemporary dancers trained in the Danish system is Erik Bruhn, famed for his noble presence.

Bournonville wrote several pedagogical guides and his followers preserved his system in six set classes, one for each day of the week except Sunday. When taught by his most fanatical disciples, these classes scarcely varied from year to year. Romanticism may have stressed the irrational and spontaneous, but, paradoxically, Romantic themes could be danced onstage only after the mastering of a rational and ordered technical system.

In a period dominated by the ballerina, Lucien Petipa, seen above with Adèle Dumilâtre in The Marble Maiden, *was one of the few male dancers to establish a firm reputation for himself. Petipa created the role of Albrecht in* Giselle, *partnering the luminous Carlotta Grisi, seen opposite in the famous* pas du songe *("dream dance") from* La Péri. *The highlight of this scene came when Grisi fell from a considerable height into her partner's outstretched arms.*

Ballet vocabulary expanded tremendously during this period, and as it did the necessity for structured teaching became apparent. One noteworthy teacher was Carlo Blasis, who became director of the Royal Academy of Dance at La Scala, Milan, in 1837. Many ballerinas studied with him, and Milanese dancers became famous for their prowess. More importantly, perhaps, Blasis taught teachers who in turn taught other teachers, thereby codifying classical ballet. Romantic choreography could be exuberant, but Blasis' teaching was sober. He often cited examples from ancient or neoclassic art, as when he made Giovanni da Bologna's bronze statue of the god Mercury the prototype for the position known as *attitude* (in which the dancer stands on one leg while the other is raised behind him with bent knee). Blasis' methodology is a reminder that ballet is a conservative art in the best sense of the term, making daring experiments in the theater but preserving its traditions in the classroom.

Of all nineteenth-century innovations, none has had a more devastating effect than dancing *en pointe*. Toe dancing is so closely associated with ballet in the popular mind that dancegoers are frequently astonished to discover that it is a relatively recent invention, one that Camargo and La Barberina never knew about for all their virtuosity. Just who did invent dancing *en pointe*—and when—remains a mystery. The use of wires in such ballets as *Zephyr and Flora* certainly helped dancers pause momentarily on their toes, and sometime before 1820 Geneviève Gosselin and Avdotia Istomina, a Russian ballerina admired by Pushkin, may have danced *en pointe* without using wires.

To dance *en pointe*, today's ballerina wears shoes with toes reinforced by layers of glue between layers of material. Early Romantic ballerinas, by contrast, wore slippers with wadding inserted inside and a little darning outside to permit a better grip on the floor. They danced *en pointe* with no other support—as any well-disciplined dancer should be able to do, for the toe shoe is no magic gimmick, it is only an aid to dancing. The secret of *pointe* work lies not in the shoe but in the per-

The copious illustrations in Carlo Blasis' seminal study of ballet, A Theoretical, Practical and Elementary Treatise on the Art of Dancing, *reflect the careful anatomical and geometrical investigation he conducted prior to writing the book. The plates above demonstrate classic attitudes, while those below show dancers during performances.*

former's correctly trained body. Among early ballerinas, Marie Taglioni, in such works as *La Sylphide*, most strikingly demonstrated how skimming *pointe* steps could suggest otherworldliness. From the beginning, such *pointe* dancing has been associated with women, and it remains a woman's way of dancing, although there is no anatomical reason why it cannot be attempted by men.

Taglioni's ethereal purity resulted from grueling training under the eyes of her father. Sometimes his classes were so exhausting that at the end of a lesson she would be nearly unconscious and would have to be undressed, sponged, and dressed again before she regained her senses. Such ruthlessness produced a ballerina who was the very incarnation of a sylph, however. She danced her way across Europe, and she even visited Russia. Returning from St. Petersburg, Taglioni's carriage was stopped by bandits. Terrified, the ballerina offered the bandit chieftain her jewels as well as her purse. He refused both, however, insisting that his only wish was to see the great Taglioni dance. Rugs were laid on the road, two accompanists tuned their violins, and Taglioni gave an impromptu recital. Afterwards, the bandit chief kept the rugs as souvenirs of the command performance but let the ballerina and her retinue go free with their belongings.

Taglioni was urged by her father to remove all hints of the carnal from her dancing, and as a result her style was often referred to as chaste. Quite different was the dancing of Fanny Elssler. Théophile Gautier, the novelist and poet who was also an important dance critic, characterized Taglioni as a "Christian" and Elssler as a "pagan" dancer. The comparison was apt, for in contrast to the spiritual Taglioni, Elssler danced with great human warmth. (Dr. Louis Véron, who became director of the Paris Opéra in 1831 and who had a shrewd eye for publicity, was to encourage the development of a Camargo-Sallé style rivalry between Taglioni and Elssler.) Among Elssler's specialties were vivacious solos based upon folk dances. She set Paris agog in 1836 when, in Jean Coralli's *Le Diable Boiteux*, she performed the "Cachu-

MARIA TAGLIONI

NEL BALLO LA GITANA

cha" in which, all voluptuousness and fire and playing castanets as she danced, she twisted and turned with a thousand bewitching gestures. The prudes professed to be shocked, yet they kept coming back to see her. In 1839 she enjoyed another success with the "Cracovienne" in Joseph Mazilier's *La Gypsy*. Here she wore boots with steel spurs and their joyous clinking suggested "castanets on the heels" to Gautier.

The most widely traveled ballerina of the time, Elssler toured both Western Europe and Russia, and she was the first great ballerina to visit the New World. In Havana, an admirer gave her a box of "cigars" made of solid gold; in Washington, Congress adjourned on the day of one of her appearances; and the euphoric Yankees christened boats, stockings, garters, corsets, shawls, parasols, fans, shoe polish, shaving soap, and champagne after her. The New England intellectuals were enthralled; at one Boston performance, Margaret Fuller turned to Ralph Waldo Emerson and said, "Ralph, this is poetry." "No," he replied, "it is religion." Nathaniel Hawthorne apparently agreed, for he hung a picture of Elssler on his wall between portraits of Ignatius Loyola and Francis Xavier.

Today, it is amusing to read that some of Elssler's fans drank champagne from her slipper and presented her with a cross made from the wood of George Washington's bier, just as it is amusing to read that Taglioni's fans in St. Petersburg ate a pair of her ballet slippers at dinner. Yet there is a disconcerting note of hysteria about these tales. Ballet was becoming a mania. In the court days it had been a male art; now it was a female art, and some devotees frankly admitted that they went to performances to ogle the *danseuses*.

The directors of the Paris Opéra were well aware of the power of feminine charms. They permitted visitors to go backstage and chat with dancers in the *foyer de la danse*, a large room next to the stage

Filippo Taglioni designed a large repertoire of ballets to showcase the multifarious talents of his daughter, Marie. At left she is seen as an amnesia-struck gypsy girl in La Gitana, *and below (at far right) as Algaë, fancifully called a "student of love." Both ballets were presented during the Taglionis' successful tour of Imperial Russia in 1837–38.*

Ballet Aglaé.

Mlle. Taglioni.   Mlle. Miss St. Romain.   Marie Mercy.   Mr. Stuhlmüller.   Mr. Taglioni, Sohn.
  Aglaé.   Venus.   Amor.   Hylas.   Adonis.

where the ballet company warmed up. In the auditorium itself, one box was nicknamed the *loge infernale*, for there sat fashionable blades more interested in *amour* than in art. As in the eighteenth century, prominent men kept dancers as mistresses—but covertly, in strict accordance with the rules of respectable morality. Baron Haussmann, the city planner who rebuilt Paris, was the lover of the dancer Francine Cellier. To avoid attracting attention, the baron had her dress like his daughter when they went out driving together. Mme Haussmann nevertheless discovered the affair, and she promptly left her husband, taking their real daughter with her.

Scandals abounded. There was, for example, the case of Caroline Forster and Elina Roland, two dancers of the Paris Opéra Ballet who sued a journalist for defamation of character after he wrote that these girls were such good friends that they not only danced in the same company but shared the same house and, on occasion, the same bed. And there was the most notorious of all nineteenth-century stars, the Irish-born woman who called herself Lola Montez. Although she acquired a knowledge of Spanish dancing, it was not as a dancer but as an adventuress that she achieved fame, and she reached the summit of her career as mistress of Ludwig I of Bavaria. Yet not all dancers were frivolous; many were clever and some were learned. One member of the Paris Opéra Ballet wrote a theological treatise, another was an expert on politics, and a third possessed considerable knowledge of medicine. In any case, there was more to life than champagne parties. Life, for a dancer, meant hard work and long hours.

Life was also perilous, the principal peril—the menace of all gaslit

Fanny Elssler, the earthy counterpart of the dreamlike Taglioni, made ethnic dances her specialty, particularly the Spanish "Cachucha," introduced in Coralli's Le Diable Boiteux *(above, left). The poster at far left announced Elssler's appearance in the title role of Perrot's* Caterina *at La Scala in 1847. An heir to the tradition of Taglioni, Emma Livry is shown in* Le Papillon *(below, right), which Taglioni came out of retirement to choreograph for her successor. In the nineteenth-century lithograph above, right, dancers appear* en pointe.

theaters—being fire. Gauzy tutus were dangerously flammable, and two promising dancers of the period were to die in horrible accidents as a result. During a performance of *The Revolt in the Harem*, Clara Webster of London's Drury Lane Theater touched an oil burner. Her dress caught fire and she rushed about the stage, costume ablaze, until a stagehand caught her and extinguished the flames. She was already fatally burned, however, and she died two days afterward. Emma Livry's fate was, if anything, worse. A protégée of Marie Taglioni, who had choreographed *Le Papillon* especially for her, Livry brushed against a lamp while rehearsing at the Paris Opéra. Like Webster, she was suddenly enveloped in flames; unlike Webster, she did not die immediately but lingered on through eight months of terrible agony. How ironic, in this context, that a key scene in *Le Papillon* depicts the heroine, turned into a magic butterfly, darting toward a torch until the flame shrivels her wings. How ironic, too, that shortly before Livry's accident the Opéra management ordered dancers to dip their costumes into a fireproof solution. Livry had refused, complaining that the treatment made her tutus look dingy.

Artistically, Romantic ballet attained its height in 1841 with the production of *Giselle* at the Paris Opéra. A work that remains beloved today, *Giselle* was the product of distinguished collaborators. The score was by Adolphe Adam, a popular composer of operas and ballets

best remembered today for the Christmas carol "O Holy Night." The scenario, based upon a legend recorded by the German poet Heinrich Heine, was written by Théophile Gautier and the skillful professional librettist Vernoy de Saint-Georges.

Giselle, like *La Sylphide*, is in two acts, each act exemplifying one of the dual aspects of Romanticism: the sunlit side in Act I, the moonlit side in Act II. The first act takes place in a Rhineland village during a vintage festival. Giselle, a lovely but frail peasant girl, is in love with a mysterious young man. Her idyll is shattered when she learns that this youth is really Albrecht, count of Silesia, and that he is affianced to a noblewoman. Overwhelmed, her reason shattered, Giselle turns in horror from her perfidious lover, tries to commit suicide, swoons, and falls dead. The second act is set before her tomb deep in a forest. Giselle's ghost is summoned from the grave by Myrthe, queen of the Wilis. These are spirits of women who, having died unhappy in love, are doomed for eternity to lead men to destruction (the term "wili" is

Veneration of the ballerina reached extraordinary heights during the Romantic period. And although many of the dancers led quiet, disciplined lives, others, such as Lola Montez (left), were notorious for their romantic adventures. More than a century after its premiere, Giselle remains a staple in ballet company repertories throughout the world. The photograph at right shows a scene from the first act of Ballet West's production of this classic work.

derived from a Slavic word for "vampire"). When the repentant Albrecht comes to place flowers on Giselle's grave, Myrthe orders her to dance him to his death. Instead, Giselle shields him until the first rays of dawn appear and the Wilis' power is broken.

Giselle was produced for a new ballerina, Carlotta Grisi. Announcements listed only one choreographer, Jean Coralli, who was recognized to be a competent craftsman, but everyone knew that a second and more gifted choreographer was also involved with the ballet. He was Jules Perrot, and at the time he was Grisi's lover—and perhaps her legal husband as well. Whatever the nature of their collaboration, Coralli and Perrot produced a masterwork. In its dramatic action and dances, *Giselle* is enormously varied. Its two acts include both rousing peasant dances and the icy dances of the Wilis, and among the rewarding solo roles are those of Albrecht, who is transformed by love and grief from a playboy into a penitent; Myrthe, the beautiful but cruel Wili queen; and Hilarion, the gruff gamekeeper who first discovers the secret of Albrecht's aristocratic origins. The title role offers the ballerina some of the greatest challenges in ballet, for it requires her to be both a consummate actress and a brilliant technician, progressing from innocence to madness in the first act, then reappearing as an impalpable spirit. As a result, the role of Giselle has always offered considerable latitude for differing interpretations. During the Romantic period for example, Grisi stressed Giselle's tender melancholy, while Elssler was acclaimed for her passionate intensity.

Perrot is a source of continual frustration for the ballet lover. He was, evidently, one of the great choreographers of his age—possibly the greatest. Yet the one work by him we possess is *Giselle*, a collaboration with someone else. Like Bournonville, Perrot was a pupil of Vestris; he was also a distinguished dancer, winning applause even when male dancing was unfashionable. His appearance was so plain, however, and his physical proportions were so peculiar that Vestris felt compelled to advise him to move rapidly in order to prevent the audience from getting a good look at him.

During his lifetime Perrot's works were universally praised for their brilliance of conception, and the choreographer was justly celebrated for giving individual attention to everyone from the ballerina to the last member of the ensemble. A man of liberal sentiments, he created convincing characters from all social classes and his heroes were frequently men of humble birth. His ballets moved swiftly, the episodes uniting mime and dance so that every moment became dramatically expressive. Some of his best works were done between 1843 and 1848 in London, where he was associated with Her Majesty's Theatre—which, under the management of Benjamin Lumley, briefly rivaled the Paris Opéra as

Although overshadowed as a choreographer by his more famous brother Marius, Lucien Petipa did compose a number of successful dramatic ballets. A highlight of his career was the Paris Opéra production of Namouna, whose climactic moment is seen at left. Perrot's divertissement, Pas de Quatre (right), which featured the four most famous ballerinas of the period—Grisi, Taglioni, Grahn, and Cerrito—dazzled London audiences fortunate enough to attend one of its few performances.

Overleaf: Young dancers in rehearsal, a candid moment preserved for posterity by French Impressionist Edgar Degas.

a ballet center. Using such stars as Grisi, Elssler, and the buxom, flamboyant Fanny Cerrito, Perrot produced two notable and very different ballets. One, *La Esmeralda* (1844), an ambitious adaptation of Victor Hugo's *Notre Dame de Paris* complete with hunchbacked Quasimodo, was, judging from the reviews, a masterpiece of gestural detail.

The second of these ballets, the *Pas de Quatre* of 1845, was only a trifle—but what a trifle! Lumley concocted the notion of having four great ballerinas—Taglioni, Cerrito, Grisi, and Grahn—appear in the same ballet, a prospect that, as the London *Times* observed, threatened "a collision that the most carelessly managed railroad could hardly hope to equal." It was Perrot's task to make each of the stars shine, but without permitting any one of them to upstage the others. To everyone's relief, rehearsals seemed to be going well until the day when Perrot rushed into Lumley's office tearing his hair and groaning that the ballet could never be produced. A quarrel had arisen over the order of the ballerinas' solos. On the theory that the last solo was the place of honor, the three younger ballerinas had ceded it to Taglioni as a gesture of respect. But who would dance penultimately? In the rehearsal room, Cerrito and Grisi were quarreling over the spot at that very instant. What was to be done?

Lumley thought a moment, then delivered a judgment worthy of Solomon. Let the dancers perform in order of age, he said, with the eldest last. When Perrot relayed this news to the ballerinas, they stopped fighting over the final solos and rehearsals continued without further ado. The *Pas de Quatre* delighted London, and Queen Victoria and Prince Albert even attended one of its performances. In our own day, Anton Dolin and Keith Lester have attempted to reconstruct Perrot's work with new choreography in the Romantic manner.

Cerrito was married to Arthur Saint-Léon, who in 1870, the year

of his death, choreographed what is considered to be the period's last great ballet, *Coppélia, or the Girl With the Enamel Eyes*. With charming music by Léo Delibes, including the first balletic use of the Hungarian czardas, the work takes a lighthearted look at Romantic yearning. Much to the annoyance of his girl friend Swanilda, a lad named Franz starts flirting with Coppélia, the aloof daughter of Dr. Coppelius, an eccentric old inventor. Sneaking into the doctor's house, Swanilda discovers that his "daughter" is only a mechanical doll. Hearing Coppelius return, she hides in the doll's alcove. Soon, Coppelius has another visitor—Franz, who wishes to court Coppélia. Dr. Coppelius drugs him and then conceives the demented scheme of making Coppélia come to life by transferring the life force from Franz into the doll. What he does not know is that Swanilda has changed places with the doll, and when she pretends to come alive she upsets the workshop. Eventually, Coppelius realizes he has been tricked and Franz discovers that he has loved an automaton.

Under Saint-Léon's direction, what might have amounted to little more than a macabre fable about the follies of infatuation became instead a witty comedy, and Giuseppina Bozzacchi sparkled as Swanilda. Then tragedy struck: the Franco-Prussian War broke out and Paris was besieged; the Opéra closed; food grew scarce, and Parisians took to dining on dogs and cats and, finally, on sewer rats. Saint-Léon died of exhaustion, and Bozzacchi died of a virulent fever on her seventeenth birthday.

The Opéra reopened in 1871, but things were no longer the same. Ballet was in decline, and even the Opéra's move, four years later, to its present sumptuous quarters, could not reverse the trend. Symptoms of decadence had long been visible, of course, and consequently this situation was not altogether unanticipated. In *Coppélia*, for example, the role of Franz was danced not by a man but by the shapely Eugénie Fiocre, whose figure looked particularly pleasant in male attire. The cult of the ballerina had attained such proportions that male dancing was ignored and ballet became an excuse for displays of pulchritude. This was the period Degas painted. It looks lovely on canvas; in reality it was often tawdry.

A comparable decline occurred elsewhere. As early as the 1850's, Benjamin Lumley complained that London audiences were demanding legs, not brains. Talented dancers continued to appear during the remainder of the century—among them the elegant Carlotta Zambelli, who made her debut at the Paris Opéra in 1894. But many could find no creative company with which to work. Thus the exquisite Adeline Genée, once she left her native Denmark, spent much of her career in English music halls.

Italian schools went on training phenomenal technicians. As for Italian choreography, that was peculiar indeed. Late-nineteenth-century Italian ballet was dominated by Luigi Manzotti, who specialized in grandiose extravaganzas. His *Sport* glorified skating, fishing, boating, horseracing, and big-game hunting, while *Amor* depicted the creation of the world, the persecution of the early Christians, and the fall of Rome. This last feat required two hundred dancers, two hundred and

Italian choreographer Luigi Manzotti became the acknowledged master of grand theatrical extravaganzas in the late 1800's. His most popular production was Excelsior, *which was performed over one hundred times the year of its premiere, 1881. Both the choreographer and a scene from the ballet graced the cover of* Il Teatro Illustrato *(right) following the opening. The picture above shows Virginia Zucchi in one of the many spectacular costumes created for Manzotti's productions.*

IL TEATRO ILLUSTRATO

PREZZI D'ABBONAMENTO: Anno I.   Marzo 1881. — N. 3.   AVVERTENZE.

EDOARDO SONZOGNO
EDITORE
Milano — Via Pasquirolo, N. 14.

TEATRO ALLA SCALA DI MILANO. — EXCELSIOR, azione coreografica di LUIGI MANZOTTI.

fifty extras, eighteen horses, two elephants, and an ox. A fervent Italian nationalist, Manzotti was the Cecil B. de Mille of his day; his spectacles extoll moral and patriotic ideals (including the Victorian faith in science and progress) and simultaneously give audiences glimpses of pretty legs. His greatest success was *Excelsior*, an 1881 celebration of human ingenuity with scenes showing the invention of the steamboat, the experiments of Alessandro Volta in his laboratory, the operations of the Washington Telegraph Office, and the building of the Suez Canal and the tunnel through Mt. Cenis. The grand finale was a "Festival of the Nations" culminating in an "Apotheosis of Light and Peace." Such productions must have been shrewdly constructed and great fun. As serious choreography, however, they were of negligible value.

Yet even as the century was drawing to a close, with lovely ballerinas displayed in vapid ballets, great choreography did exist, not in Paris or London, but far away in Russia. As Paris dimmed, St. Petersburg became ballet's star in the north.

Lago de Cegini

5

Russia's Imperial Ballet

THE CURTAIN RISES; the scene is Egypt. An English nobleman and his comic servant John Bull, who are on an expedition to Africa, seek shelter inside a pyramid during a sandstorm. To pass the time, the Englishman decides to smoke opium. After a few puffs on the pipe he finds himself transported back into the past, where he becomes Ta-Hor, a handsome youth who saves Aspicia, the pharaoh's daughter, from a lion. Inevitably, they fall in love. But Aspicia has been promised to the Nubian king, who pursues the star-crossed lovers along the Nile. When he tries to seize Aspicia, she leaps into the river.

The scene now changes to the bottom of the Nile, where the River Spirit summons the great rivers of the world to dance before Aspicia. Restored to the land, Aspicia tells her father how the Nubian king importuned her, and she and Ta-Hor are allowed to marry. Suddenly the opium dream is ended; Ta-Hor is a Victorian gentleman again. The curtain falls. And what was that?

That was *The Daughter of Pharaoh*, choreographed by Marius Petipa and performed for the first time in St. Petersburg in 1862. A ludicrous flop? On the contrary, the ballet was wildly popular. It was danced for decades, and elderly, retired ballerinas still live who swear that it was one of the treasures of Russian ballet. Their assertions are reminders that ballet is an art of movement and that many situations that might seem peculiar from a literary standpoint are valid, even eloquent, when expressed choreographically.

The roots of Russian ballet are deep. As in Western Europe, productions combining dance with speech and song arose during the seventeenth and eighteenth centuries, which was Russia's first period of intensive Westernization. And because Russians were avidly imitating European fashions at the time, they imported many foreign ballet masters. A Frenchman, Jean Baptiste Landé, founded the St. Petersburg School of Ballet in 1738, but dance did not receive official patronage until 1766, when Catherine II established the Directorate of the Imperial Theaters, which had charge over opera, drama, and ballet. In 1806 the directorate was extended to Moscow, where Filippo Beccari had organized a dancing school at the Moscow Orphanage in 1764. Its students appeared at the Petrovsky Theater, a predecessor of the Bolshoi, and in 1784 the orphanage school was formally turned over to the Petrovsky's managers.

Italian ballerina Pierina Legnani spent eight years as a guest artist at the Imperial Theater in St. Petersburg. During that time she danced most of the key roles in the Russian repertory, including the part of Odette-Odile in the 1895 production of Swan Lake. *The photograph opposite shows Legnani as the Swan Queen.*

One early native-born choreographer was Ivan Valberkh, who specialized in melodramas—including anti-Napoleonic ballets inspired by the invasion of 1812. The major choreographers working in Russia during the nineteenth century continued to be foreign, however. Didelot, for example, came to St. Petersburg from Paris in 1801, expecting his appointment to be only temporary. Yet except for one short interruption, he stayed there until his death in 1837, doing much to improve Russian dancing. Perrot staged ballets in St. Petersburg during the 1840's and 1850's, and he in turn was succeeded by Saint-Léon. Although he remained for a decade, the latter was never totally successful. Critics found his works superficial, and his most ambitious attempt to utilize Russian folklore, *The Little Humpbacked Horse*, angered rather than pleased the intelligentsia, who apparently considered it too French.

Unquestionably the most important of the foreign choreographers was the French-born Marius Petipa, who arrived in St. Petersburg in 1847 to serve as *premier danseur*. Like Didelot, he probably thought his appointment a short-term one; instead, he remained with the Imperial Theaters for almost sixty years and became the virtual dictator of Russian ballet. Petipa had been born into a family of itinerant dancers, and in his youth he toured with his parents, dancing wherever work could be found. (In Antwerp, one of the many cities the Petipas played, the family found itself booked into a theater without lamps. Unwilling to cancel the performance, they stuck candles into potatoes and went on with the show.) Throughout his youth, Petipa danced in numerous cities, among them Paris. There, however, he was overshadowed by his brother Lucien, the first Albrecht in *Giselle*. Determined to make a name for himself independent of his brother's reputation, Petipa moved

Although Catherine the Great (above, left) was an enthusiastic supporter of all the arts, she had special affection for the ballet. Among the fruits of her patronage was a dancing school, officially opened in 1776, where noblemen's daughters such as the one shown above could receive training. Moscow's famed Bolshoi Theater, seen in the engraving at left, below, has functioned as an important center of Russian dance since its opening in 1825.

to Russia, where he assisted both Perrot and Saint-Léon. Although he had choreographed previously, his initial success came with *The Daughter of Pharaoh*, and it came because ballerina Carolina Rosati suddenly and unexpectedly requested a new production. The theater management insisted that there was no time in which to prepare one, but Petipa, rising to the challenge, managed to stage his five-hour extravaganza on less than six weeks' notice. Clearly, he was a fellow worth encouraging, and when Saint-Léon departed in 1869, Petipa was placed in full charge of the St. Petersburg ballet.

The theatrical milieu in which he worked was unique in the world, for Russian theaters were state theaters in the most literal sense of the term. Their directors were personally appointed by the tsar and all performers were in a sense imperial servants. The imperial family often attended ballet rehearsals and awarded prizes at ballet school graduations. At performances, the men in the audience remained standing until the tsar arrived and, out of respect, did not leave the theater until after he had departed. Curtain calls followed a ritual in which the ballerina bowed first to the tsar's box, then to that of the theater director, and only afterward to the general public.

Dancers remained a morally suspect lot in Western Europe, but in Russia, under imperial patronage, they gained considerable respect. Students at the state ballet schools were considered akin to those at the military or naval academies. The boys even wore similar uniforms, but whereas the naval cadet had an anchor and the prospective army officer crossed sabers on his collar, the insignia of the ballet student was Apollo's lyre. Dancing was a particularly desirable profession for women, since it combined job security with the then-rare opportunity to lead an independent life.

By the middle of the nineteenth century, ballet companies thrived in both Moscow and St. Petersburg. In the old capital performances were held at the Bolshoi Theater; in St. Petersburg, at both the Bolshoi and Maryinsky theaters, until the former was declared structurally unsafe and ballet was confined to the latter (now called the Kirov). The companies were rivals then, as they are today—St. Petersburg dancers accused their Moscow colleagues of crude flamboyance while Muscovites branded St. Petersburg "academic."

It was in St. Petersburg, then, that ballet prospered under Petipa. The city prided itself on its elegance, its baroque palaces amid formal gardens and imposing avenues reminding some visitors of an icebound Rome. The Maryinsky, with its handsome chandeliers and its color scheme of white, gold, and peacock blue, was as elegant as the city in which it stood. In some ways it resembled a private club, since most of the seats were reserved for nobles, diplomats, and prominent merchants and bankers. Some fans faithfully attended every ballet performance. These were the balletomanes, for whom dancing was almost an addiction. They followed the career of every dancer and were familiar with the details of every ballet, but their taste tended to be conservative and they often exerted a retrograde influence.

Portraits of Marius Petipa in his maturity depict a courtly gentleman with medals pinned to his chest. He looks like a diplomat, and indeed

65

he was something of a diplomat, capable of pleasing the public and the official bureaucracy without totally compromising his artistry. He also suggests certain film directors who manage to combine genius with commercial shrewdness. As a result, Petipa is a complex person to discuss. He decidedly shared the sentimental taste of his time, and some of his dances were pure kitsch. In *The Blue Dahlia*, for instance, a ballerina with a sprinkling can waters a flowerbed that turns into a group of dancers, and *The Magic Pills* contains a game scene in which the dancers are dressed as playing cards and dominoes. Furthermore, Petipa's compositional procedures were extremely cut-and-dried. Instead of searching for inspiration, he devised groupings at home, using figures resembling chessmen. He liked to have dances "on reserve," numbers that he could automatically fit into any ballet that required an extra dance, no matter what its ostensible theme might be. Putting works together on a theatrical assembly line, he often had assistants choreograph scenes for him—particularly ones with dances for men, since he was seldom interested in male dancing—and he always gave composers meticulous instructions about what sort of music he needed. He collaborated splendidly with Peter Tchaikovsky and Alexander Glazunov, but was equally happy with the lilting but seldom distinguished tunes of such workmanlike composers as Cesare Pugni and Leon Minkus.

Visually, Petipa's productions were strange. Although minor characters usually wore costumes suggesting the ballet's particular period or locale, the stars wore conventionalized dancing costumes. Anachronisms abounded. Thus Aspicia in *The Daughter of Pharaoh* wore a classical tutu with a lotus design upon it to remind audiences that she was Egyptian. Likewise, the ballerina in a Spanish work might also wear a tutu; only the rose in her hair would indicate that the setting was Seville. Often the star appeared in her favorite coiffure, and even if she portrayed a slave she still might wear a prized pearl necklace. Nevertheless, Petipa was a genius, ranking with Perrot and Bournonville among the great nineteenth-century choreographers. To understand that genius one must come to terms with the way Petipa structured his ballets.

The typical Petipa ballet stretched out its narrative over three or four acts, even when the story might conceivably be told more concisely. Somewhere toward the end of the ballet occurred a *divertissement*, a suite of dances that had no direct connection with the plot but was inserted—as the name suggests—primarily to divert. Usually, some pretext for it could be found; the performers represented guests at a wedding or visitors to a castle. Essentially, however, the *divertissement* existed simply as a collection of sparkling dances. Also toward the end of the ballet there was a spectacular *pas de deux*—a duet for the ballerina and her partner. This *pas de deux* usually developed according to a strict form: first came a stately section (the adagio) for both performers, emphasizing lyrical and sustained movements. Then came two solos (called "variations"), the first for the man, the second for the ballerina. Finally, in the coda, the stars appeared together again, the choreography emphasizing quick, flashy steps. If the *pas de deux* form could degenerate into formula, it nonetheless permitted adroit displays of male and female movement. No wonder choreographers still remain fond of it.

Dancer-choreographer-designer Marius Petipa's costumes for The Daughter of Pharaoh *were a curious mixture of authentic period design and classical ballet attire. Petipa, who personally performed the leading role in the ballet, is seen at left in ersatz Arab garb as the character Ta-Hor, an Egyptian youth. In a later revival, ballerina Julia Sedova (below, left) wore a conventional tutu distinguished only by its lotus motif. Petipa created* Pharaoh, *his first choreographic triumph, in a mere six weeks—to satisfy a request by prima ballerina Carolina Rosati (below) for a new vehicle for her talents.*

Petipa ballets contained many different kinds of dancing. In Russia and Western Europe, labels existed for some of them. Classical dancing derived from the pure ballet vocabulary and was reserved for the hero and heroine, or for dancers representing fairies or spirits. Character (or *caractère*) dance was based upon folk forms such as the mazurka, czardas, or tarantella. (The term could also be applied to movement expressive of certain occupations, social classes, or individual eccentricities.) In addition, there was *demi-caractère* dance, which flavored classicism with piquant touches of character dance. Soubrette roles, such as that of Swanilda in *Coppélia*, were often *demi-caractère*.

Then there was mime, a system of gestures that helped tell the story. Quite unlike modern stage action, these gestures were as codified as the sign language for the deaf. Some were obvious enough: hand on heart meant love; shaking one's fists above one's head represented anger. Others seem arbitrary: hands circling around each other above the head symbolized dance, while to circle one's face with one's hand indicated that the person referred to was beautiful.

Filled with mime, dramatic dance, lyric dance, classical dance, character dance, and *divertissements*, Petipa's ballets were essentially panoramic. Although leisurely, these productions contained a richness and variety of movement that allowed them to go on for hours without turning monotonous. Petipa constructed whole universes of movement in which each separate dance glittered like a star yet formed part of a harmonious whole. Indeed, glittering is a good adjective to describe Petipa's works, for he replaced the softness and fragility of Romantic ballet with a diamond-edged sharpness. Endlessly inventive, Petipa created gratifying dances for soloists and ensembles alike. Because of this ability, his anachronisms are relatively unimportant. Just as no one seriously criticizes Shakespeare because the historical Antony and Cleopatra never spoke blank verse, so no one really condemns Petipa for putting ancient Egyptians into tutus. Both merely utilized conventions that facilitated, rather than hindered, artistic expression.

Some of Petipa's effects remain impressive even today. One such piece is the "Kingdom of the Shades" episode from *La Bayadère*, choreographed in 1877. In the realm of the dead, a young man seeks his beloved. One by one the ghosts enter, each in a white tutu. Identically dressed, they perform identical steps. The first girl steps forward and extends one leg in a straight line behind her. Then she lowers her leg from the *arabesque*, as the pose is called, steps forward, and assumes an identical pose. Meanwhile, another girl has appeared behind her, joining the forward progression, while behind her a third and fourth dancer have taken their places. By the time thirty or more dancers have appeared, the spectator finds himself in a state of mystic calm induced by these choreographic repetitions.

Given the expansiveness of Petipa's structure, plots ranged from the florid drama of *The Daughter of Pharaoh* to situations serving as mere frames for the dances. Don Quixote is only a subordinate character in the exuberant ballet of that name, for example, and as for *Raymonda*, no one has ever been interested in its story of how a Crusader saves the heroine from a Saracen. What makes *Raymonda* an enduring favorite are its dances, which blend classicism with Hungarian folk steps. In these works Petipa developed the purely kinetic, as distinct from the dramatic, elements of dancing to such an extent that drama and dance became almost separate entities.

The Sleeping Beauty surely ranks as Petipa's most resplendent production. As was customary, Petipa sent Tchaikovsky musical specifications based upon the scenario by Ivan Vsevolojsky, the director of the Imperial Theaters. Far from objecting to these specifications, Tchaikovsky thrived on them, and he produced a masterful score. Yet when the tsar heard it at a gala dress rehearsal before its 1890 premiere, his sole comment was a polite but unenthusiastic, "Very nice." Tchaikovsky was hurt, but the ballet became a towering success.

Judged as a play, the scenario for *The Sleeping Beauty* is long-winded and not enough seems to happen in each of its acts. In the prologue, the witch Carabosse predicts that the newborn Princess Aurora will someday prick her finger on a spinning needle and die, but the Lilac Fairy immediately modifies the curse so that Aurora will only sink into a trancelike sleep. This eventually happens when, during the celebration of Aurora's sixteenth birthday, she plays with a spindle. A century later, the Lilac Fairy reveals the slumbering Aurora to a prince in a vision and then leads him to her. Aurora awakens at his kiss, and the last act is their wedding.

A play could certainly say twice as much in half the time, but a ballet is not a play and it makes a statement purely through movement. In this regard the movement in *The Sleeping Beauty* is unusual in its visual beauty and thematic implications. With its regal processions, it both glorifies monarchy—an implied flattery that the tsar was not quick enough to grasp—and celebrates the virtues of dignity, courtliness, and fine manners, which remain relevant even in an age without tsars. In addition, Petipa depicts the growth of a woman from childhood to maturity. At her birthday party, Aurora is an innocent girl, courted by four cavaliers in the so-called Rose Adagio. This dance requires her to sustain difficult balances without visible strain while suitors present her with roses. More than a stunt, the adagio is a ceremony of courtship in which Aurora is an object of adoration. Later, in the vision scene, she appears before the prince as an incarnation of the elusive Romantic ideal. But when her slumber is broken, she is a fully human woman awakened to love. The work's essential opulence is reinforced in each act by the dances. The prologue contains distinctive variations for each of the fairies at Aurora's christening, while the last act *divertissement*, which involves such fairy-tale characters as Puss in Boots and Little Red Riding Hood, culminates in two splendid *pas de deux*: a swift, fluttering one for a bluebird and an enchanted princess, and an expansive one for Aurora and her prince.

Petipa's ballets required excellent dancers, and the Imperial School assembled a worthy faculty. Distinguished teachers included Pavel Gerdt, the noblest of Russian male dancers; Christian Johannsen, a Bournonville pupil whose class was rightly termed "the class of perfection;" and Enrico Cecchetti, an Italian virtuoso whose class fostered the brilliance produced by Italian academies. As a result, of course, the

Extended exposure to the artistry and technique of such foreign-born artists as Virginia Zucchi (right) had a profound impact upon native Russian ballet during the nineteenth century—a period that witnessed the creation of Petipa's The Sleeping Beauty *and Petipa and Ivanov's* Swan Lake. *Impervious to changing tastes, Ivanov's* The Nutcracker, *(performed below with revised choreography by the Bolshoi Ballet) remains a part of Christmas celebrations in many countries throughout the world.*

Overleaf: *Pierina Legnani stunned St. Petersburg audiences by completing thirty-two fouettés (whipping turns on one foot) during a performance of* Cinderella—*a feat she was to repeat in the third act of* Swan Lake. *The ballerina's technical brilliance is recreated in the sequence of time-exposure photographs.*

Russian style incorporated some of the best features of the French, Danish, and Italian traditions. Another incentive spurring dancers on to greater accomplishments was the influence of guest ballerinas from Italy. The first of them, Virginia Zucchi, charmed audiences with her expressive dramatic power, while others—including Pierina Legnani and Carlotta Brianza—were noted for their technical dazzle.

Of Petipa's associates, the most enigmatic is surely the Russian-born Lev Ivanov. An introspective man of great charm, Ivanov was somewhat lackadaisical, exerting himself too little and possibly drinking a bit too much. He occasionally choreographed scenes at the Maryinsky for which Petipa later took most of the credit, and this may have been Ivanov's problem. He lived constantly under Petipa's shadow, and there is no way of knowing how good a choreographer he might have been had he not felt himself thwarted. That question remains unanswerable, but there is no question of Ivanov's genius, for he choreographed *The Nutcracker* and much of *Swan Lake*.

The Nutcracker really belonged to Petipa, for it was he who sent the musical requirements to Tchaikovsky and it was he who was preparing to stage this fantasy about a little girl's Christmas dream of the land of the Sugar Plum Fairy. But Petipa became ill in 1892, and thus Ivanov came to choreograph *The Nutcracker*—following Petipa's instructions but inventing his own steps. Possibly because Ivanov was hampered by someone else's production scheme, his choreography was uneven, although a swirling dance for snowflakes and a stately *pas de deux* were praised. Although constantly revised by other choreographers, *The Nutcracker* survives as the world's favorite Christmas ballet. Its appeal is simple, yet profound. The first act, a Christmas party, conjures up everyone's notions of what a happy home should be like, while the second act, the little girl's dream, is a pure flight of fancy.

Swan Lake, the earliest ballet that Tchaikovsky composed, was the last to gain success. Produced initially by the Moscow Bolshoi in 1877, it suffered from mediocre choreography and its music was said to be "too Wagnerian." A later version fared scarcely better, but following the success of *The Sleeping Beauty* and *The Nutcracker* there was talk about a St. Petersburg production. Then Tchaikovsky died of cholera in 1893. For a memorial concert the following year Ivanov choreographed *Swan Lake's* second act, and the complete ballet was presented in 1895 with the first and third acts by Petipa and the second and fourth by Ivanov.

Unlike some Maryinsky ballets, *Swan Lake* is dramatically taut. It tells of Prince Siegfried, who goes hunting by a misty lake where he encounters the beautiful swan queen, Odette. She explains that she is under a magician's spell that can be broken only if a man remains faithful to her. Siegfried swears to do so, but at a ball he meets Odile, the magician's daughter disguised as Odette, and promises to marry her. Realizing her trickery, he returns to the lake to be near Odette. Various stagings differ from this point onward: in some, Siegfried defeats the magician in combat, while in others the lovers plunge into the lake and are eternally united in the afterworld. In any case, love triumphs over deception.

Each act contains felicities, but Ivanov's lakeside scenes are particularly memorable. Limpid, tender, and almost ecstatically lyrical, they contrast strikingly with the scenes of Siegfried's court, which Petipa choreographed. Petipa's most stunning contribution is the Black Swan *pas de deux*, in which Odile tries to convince Siegfried that she is Odette. The roles of Odette and Odile, usually portrayed by the same dancer, constitute a kind of Jekyll-Hyde challenge for the ballerina. During their *pas de deux*, Odile entices Siegfried with thirty-two whipping turns known as *fouettés*. The *fouetté* was one of the specialties of Pierina Legnani, the first Odette-Odile. Earlier, she had amazed everyone by introducing them into Petipa's *Cinderella*. Recognizing their effectiveness, Petipa used the *fouettés* in *Swan Lake*. Today, as in the past, many fans count the *fouettés* to make sure that the ballerina does the canonical number.

For a long time, Russian dancers had been unable to achieve *fouettés*. The secret, learned in her Italian studio, belonged to Legnani, and naturally enough she was not eager to divulge it. Thus it was not until a Russian ballerina, Mathilde Kchessinska, discovered that in order to spin without losing balance one had to have a visible fixed point before one's eyes with every turn that the *fouetté* was mastered. As her fixed point, Kchessinska selected the medals on the chest of a baron who always sat in the same seat—and she whirled and whirled away, thereby proving that Russian dancers could equal any visiting Italians. Kchessinska also belongs to political history—for she was the mistress of Tsar Nicholas II before his accession to the throne, and after the Revolution she married Nicholas's cousin, the Grand Duke André. Moreover, it was from Kchessinska's balcony that Lenin delivered his first public speech upon gaining power.

By the early twentieth century, Russian ballet was the world's finest, at least technically speaking. Creatively, things had started to go

The imperial ballets of Moscow and St. Petersburg lent many of their finest performers to Sergei Diaghilev's Paris-based Ballets Russes. Both Sophie Fedorova of Moscow (below, left) and Ludmilla Schollar of St. Petersburg (opposite) appeared during the 1911 season. Mathilde Kchessinska (above) was the first of the Russian prima ballerinas to discover the secret technique that was employed by Italian dancers in achieving fouettés.

stale; too many productions followed hidebound patterns, and dancers grew increasingly restive. One, Alexander Gorsky, trained in St. Petersburg before going to Moscow in 1898 to work with the Bolshoi Ballet, which was in the doldrums. Impressed by the realism of Stanislavski's Moscow Art Theater, Gorsky revised the Petipa repertoire, breaking up Petipa's rigid ensembles and introducing additional stage business. It is difficult for non-Russians to appraise Gorsky. He unquestionably revitalized the Bolshoi, but what we have seen of his Petipa revisions often seems bothersome tinkering, neither reverent enough to be authentic Petipa nor free enough to be a totally new conception.

St. Petersburg was the home of another young reformer, Michel Fokine, who was more interested in creating new ballets than in rechoreographing old. Early in his career Fokine concluded that ballet should be an artistic unity, that outmoded conventions should be discarded, and that every moment of a ballet should be expressive. What he was doing was rephrasing Noverre's theories into terms appropriate for twentieth-century Russia. The reactionaries opposed him, yet after a performance of Fokine's *The Vine* in 1906, Petipa sent the young man a note which began, "*Cher Camarade*," and concluded, "You will be a great ballet master."

That prophecy came true. Alert and inquisitive, Fokine associated with the artistically liberal members of the St. Petersburg intelligentsia. Among them was a dilettante named Sergei Diaghilev, who, although he had edited an art magazine and had organized exhibitions and concerts, had not really found his place in life. Soon he would be directing a ballet company with Fokine as principal choreographer, a company that helped bring about radical changes in the art of dance.

BAKST

SAISON RUSSE 1909

OPERA ET BALLET

6

Rebels and Revolutionaries

"ASTONISH ME, JEAN," ballet director Sergei Diaghilev once advised the young artist and writer Jean Cocteau. Those words say a great deal, both about Diaghilev and about twentieth-century art, for modern artists have loved to astonish. At worst, this has resulted in strident attempts to shock jaded sophisticates; at best, the attitude underlying Diaghilev's advice has emphasized the excitement and energy of art, the ways in which modern art—including dance—has dared to be the enemy of complacency.

The individual most responsible for making twentieth-century dance an astonishing art form was Diaghilev. He was neither a dancer nor a choreographer, yet as a company director he had intelligence, willpower, and, above all, taste. During its twenty-year existence, Diaghilev's Ballets Russes offered new scores by Stravinsky, Prokofiev, Ravel, Debussy, Richard Strauss, Satie, Falla, Milhaud, and Poulenc; designs by Picasso, Bakst, Benois, Derain, Braque, Utrillo, Miró, Matisse, Tchelitchew, di Chirico, and Rouault; and choreography by no less than five major talents—Michel Fokine, Vaslav Nijinsky, Léonide Massine, Bronislava Nijinska, and George Balanchine.

Having previously presented opera abroad, Diaghilev was encouraged by a friend, designer Alexandre Benois, to export Russian ballet to Western Europe. During the first of these ballet seasons, in 1909, the dancers included stars from St. Petersburg and Moscow, among them Anna Pavlova, Tamara Karsavina, Yekaterina Geltzer, Vera Karalli, Vaslav Nijinsky, Mikhail Mordkin, and Adolph Bolm. Initially, the company was regarded not as a permanent institution but as a showcase for dancers from the established theaters. With success, however, Diaghilev's Ballets Russes became increasingly independent, eventually achieving complete autonomy.

Ever the showman, Diaghilev determined to make his company's Paris debut memorable. He redecorated the large but shabby Théâtre du Châtelet, scrubbing and painting it, laying new carpets and improving the lighting. To provide additional glamour, he sent complimentary tickets to the most beautiful actresses in Paris and sat them in the first row of the balcony. But the real impact of opening night, May 19, 1909, had more to do with artistic excellence than with publicity stunts. When the curtain fell on hordes of warriors leaping ferociously in the Polovetsian dances from Alexander Borodin's *Prince Igor*, the delirious

LES BALLETS RUSSES
PROGRAMME ÉDITÉ PAR
COMŒDIA ILLUSTRÉ

Prix :
2 francs

NIJINSKY
dans "La Péri"

Aquarelle de Léon BAKST.

BAKST
1911

audience rushed down the aisle and tore off the orchestra rail in an effort to embrace the dancers.

All of Diaghilev's early triumphs—including the Polovetsian dances—were choreographed by Fokine. At the Maryinsky, where his career had begun, the rebellious Fokine had encountered entrenched bureaucrats and reactionary balletomanes, and it was not until he joined the Diaghilev company that his creative genius bloomed. Audiences used to the anemic performances of the Paris Opéra Ballet found Fokine's creations wondrously exotic. *Firebird*, set to Stravinsky's first ballet score, possessed the mysteriousness of ancient folklore. *Schéhérazade* was scandalous, featuring an orgy in a seraglio. Léon Bakst's extravagant setting for this ballet was an orgy in itself, and the richness of the back-

Although Bakst prepared both costume sketches and theater programs (left) for a Ballets Russes production of La Péri, the work was never staged by the company. In 1910 Diaghilev's troupe offered Firebird, *a reworking of several familiar Russian folktales that marked Igor Stravinsky's debut as a composer of ballet scores. The ubiquitous Bakst did costume designs for the* Firebird *(right), but the rest of the production was handled by his extremely able colleague, Alexander Golovine.*

drops had great influence upon fashion and interior decoration, prompting a vogue for vibrant colors. In *Cléopâtre*, yet another of Fokine's successes, the Queen of Egypt made an entrance audiences never forgot: she was carried onstage in a sarcophagus, her body wrapped in veils like a mummy. When the veils were removed, Cleopatra stood revealed in all her beauty. Then there was *Petrouchka*, set to another Stravinsky score, the pathetic tale of a puppet who comes to life only to prove unlucky in love amidst the swirl of a Russian carnival.

Such dance dramas demonstrated that ballet could express complex emotions. They also elevated male roles, which at the Paris Opéra were often danced by women, until they were equal in prominence to those for the ballerinas, thereby giving productions added vitality. Most importantly, Fokine's ballets were tightly organized. The full-evening ballet bored Fokine—who felt that the multiact ballet, except when choreographed by a genius such as Petipa, tended to be a stylistic hodgepodge—and he advocated ballets that presented unified artistic images. The taut works which resulted were so compelling that in Western Europe and America, in particular, the one-act ballet supplanted the evening-long ballet as the choreographic norm.

Fokine realized that in the old, multiact ballets dramatic sequences were almost totally separate from dances of atmosphere or of purely physical and technical beauty; he simply made the separation complete. For most of his career, Fokine concentrated upon dramatic ballets, but he also produced plotless pieces, the most beloved of which he called *Les Sylphides* in honor of the first great Romantic ballet. But *Les Sylphides* is more than nostalgia; it is a crucial piece of modern choreography since it demonstrates that movement can exist as a beautiful thing in itself, apart from narrative. By proving that a dramatic situation is not necessary as an excuse for dancing, Fokine freed choreographers from the necessity of padding their ballets with *divertissements*. If drama is what the choreographer wants, then he can make every moment of his creation dramatic. Abstract ballet begins with *Les Sylphides*, but *Les Sylphides* has also influenced the course of dance drama.

Despite his achievements, Fokine soon left the Ballets Russes. The reasons why are complex. Diaghilev loved novelty—including new choreographers—and as a result members of his company were in constant danger of being pronounced obsolete. Moreover, Diaghilev's infatuations could be simultaneously aesthetic and personal. He made little attempt to conceal his homosexuality—he once chided some male colleagues for possessing "a morbid interest in women"—and in his company's early years he was infatuated with Vaslav Nijinsky.

Offstage, Nijinsky was a short, thickset, rather shy young man with vaguely Mongolian features. Onstage, he was electrifying—and apparently protean. As Petrouchka he seemed lumpy, stuffed with straw; as the Favorite Slave in *Schéhérazade* he became part serpent, part panther; in more conventionally classical roles he possessed a remarkable elevation that Fokine emphasized in *Spectre de la Rose*. Portraying the spirit of a rose brought home by a girl after a ball, he appeared in her bedroom like a waking dream and then, in the most famous leap in all of ballet, soared out her window into the night.

The object of immense adoration throughout his brief career, Vaslav Nijinsky (above) was deified by his fans following the premier danseur's forced retirement. Foremost among Nijinsky's admirers was Diaghilev himself (above, right), and it was he who encouraged the shy, young dancer to try his hand at choreography. The resulting dances were highly idiosyncratic and unexpectedly provocative—and one in particular, Le Sacre du Printemps, provoked a riot when it was premiered in 1913. The photograph at right was taken during a performance of Le Sacre given by the Ballets Russes in 1920. By that time Nijinsky had been declared insane, his choreography had been forgotten, and Léonide Massine had restaged the once-controversial ballet.

But Diaghilev was not content for Nijinsky to be his company's male star. He also wanted him to be a choreographer—and this competition angered Fokine. Nijinsky, though a slow worker, managed to stage several works, each of them controversial. His only surviving ballet, set to Debussy's *Afternoon of a Faun*, created an uproar because of its alleged obscenity when it was premiered in 1912. In the ballet's most provocative scene, a nymph runs from an amorous faun, dropping a scarf in her flight. He finds it and slowly lies down on it—a gesture dark with suggestions of both masturbation and fetishism. However moral or immoral this ballet may be, it remains peculiar to behold: in contrast to Debussy's lush music, Nijinsky's choreography favors straight lines and angles. Movements are turned in, and poses suggest Greek friezes or vase paintings.

Nijinsky used a Debussy score again for *Jeux*, a 1913 ballet concerning a flirtation between three young tennis players. One of this work's novelties was its contemporary setting, which served as a reminder that ballet need not confine itself to fantasy or remote historical periods. *Jeux* might have made a greater stir if it had not been eclipsed by another Nijinsky premiere that season, *Le Sacre du Printemps*, which touched off a riot at the Théâtre des Champs-Elysées. As soon as the first notes of Stravinsky's music were sounded, the hubbub began. Fistfights developed between Stravinsky's supporters and opponents, and the pandemonium became so great that, although the score is notoriously loud, the dancers could not hear the music and

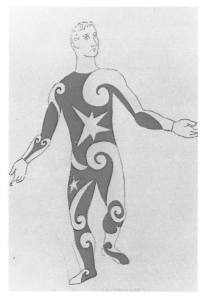

Nijinsky had to stand in the wings pounding out the rhythms. The music's strangeness caused most of the commotion, but the choreography was equally unconventional. Depicting rites in which a Chosen Maiden dances herself to death to propitiate the gods, the ballet—despite its pagan Russian setting—hinted at primordial forces that lie buried in everyone. Like many Diaghilev productions, *Le Sacre du Printemps* demonstrated that ballet could incorporate nonclassical, even violently anticlassical, movement and emerge as a richer art, one that preserved its foundations in tradition.

Nijinsky would probably have continued to choreograph for the Ballets Russes, but in 1913 he chose to marry, and a stung and embittered Diaghilev dismissed him. Nijinsky was later rehired, but he was no longer Diaghilev's favorite. Over the next few years his behavior grew increasingly strange. He sometimes refused to perform at all, he developed a fear of falling through trapdoors, and he accused other dancers of trying to injure him. At last it became apparent to all concerned that the dancer was mentally ill, and in 1917 his stage career came to an end.

Diaghilev found a new protégé in Léonide Massine, who became an extraordinary choreographer and a fine character dancer as well. Massine's ballets were witty and sophisticated, alive with quirky gestures that verged upon grotesquerie and caricature. Among his successes were *The Good-Humored Ladies*, in the style of eighteenth-century comedy; *The Three-Cornered Hat*, a robust story of how a miller's wife saves herself from the unwanted attentions of a haughty governor; and *La Boutique Fantasque*, a ballet on the ever-popular theme of dolls coming to life.

With these productions, Diaghilev's company underwent a change. Early Diaghilev seasons impressed Western audiences with their Russian exoticism and primitivism. But Diaghilev was not content to be a mere purveyor of the picturesque. In any case, the Revolution now separated him and his company from Russia. Cosmopolitan in taste, he therefore made his ballet artistically cosmopolitan, turning to Cubist or

Léonide Massine's long career began in 1914 with the Ballets Russes, for which he made his first ballet, The Midnight Sun, *a year later. With Nijinsky's departure from the company, Massine became its principal choreographer, a position consolidated in 1917 by the success of* Parade. *A fanciful Picasso costume for an acrobat (above, right) differs markedly in style from the sideshow manager's costume in the Joffrey Ballet's revival of* Parade *(above, left), But Diaghilev quarreled with Massine, and Nijinsky's sister, Bronislava Nijinska, later replaced him. In* Les Noces *(right), Nijinska's choreography was executed to Stravinsky's chants, wails, and shouts for a massed chorus.*

Surrealist painters for scenery and to experimental composers for music. Conservative historians occasionally frown upon these developments, yet if it is true that Diaghilev was guilty of faddism, his interest in the culture of his time was surely laudable. From World War I onward his company was emphatically internationalist in every respect but one; the personnel remained largely Russian, and when dancers from other countries were hired they were expected to adopt Slavic names. Among Diaghilev's later stars were Alicia Markova, Anton Dolin, and Lydia Sokolova. Despite their names, all three were British. Such changing of names may have had an inadvertent detrimental influence, for it encouraged audiences to feel that Russia held a monopoly on dance talent, and as a result attempts to form native American or English ballet companies were greeted with scorn.

A typical product of Diaghilev's modernism was *Parade*. Massine's choreography for this 1917 ballet concerned sideshow acts at a Parisian fair—but the managers of the entertainers wore, as costumes, huge skyscraperlike Cubist constructions designed by Picasso, and Satie's music included the sounds of typewriters and steamship whistles. During the 1920's Diaghilev produced several topical works that have been dubbed "choreographic cocktails," including two satires on the

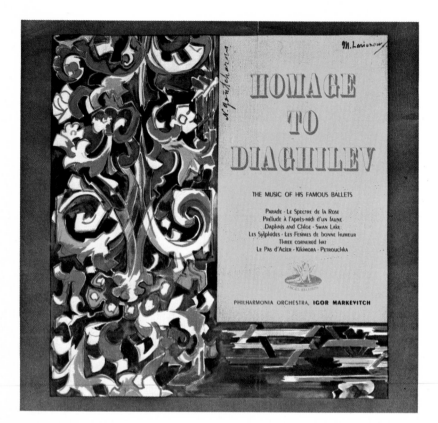

Riviera smart set, *Les Biches* and *Le Train Bleu*, both choreographed by Bronislava Nijinska. By then Diaghilev and Massine had quarreled, and Diaghilev turned for productions to Nijinska, Vaslav's sister and a distinguished artist in her own right. Her masterpiece proved to be *Les Noces*, danced to Stravinsky's cantata about a Russian peasant wedding. Instead of devising exuberant folk dances, Nijinska filled the stage with monumental groupings to convey the awesomeness of religious sacraments and of the natural cycle of growth and regeneration.

Diaghilev's last choreographer was George Balanchine. Trained in St. Petersburg, Balanchine was touring Western Europe with a Soviet dance group when Diaghilev hired him in 1924. Over the next four years, Balanchine was to choreograph ten productions for Diaghilev, only two of which survive. *The Prodigal Son* retells the biblical parable in an expressionistic fashion, its strangest scenes being those of the prodigal's dissipation. The revelers' dances seem almost mechanical, as though Balanchine were trying to show that when sensuality degenerates into debauchery it becomes a compulsive, debilitating condition like alcoholism or drug addiction. In contrast, *Apollo* depicts the birth of the god and his encounters with three muses. Gawky at first, the young Apollo grows increasingly noble as the ballet proceeds and he learns to be worthy of his own divinity.

Throughout its existence, Diaghilev's company was dominated by its director. It was his company in the same sense that the court ballet of St. Petersburg had been the tsar's company. Indeed, with his mono-

cle and the white streak in his hair that earned him the nickname "Chinchilla," Diaghilev somewhat resembled a monarch. But being ballet's monarch was not easy, for although his company mounted lavish productions and was adored by chic socialites, it was also constantly threatened by bankruptcy—and consequently Diaghilev was never free of financial worry.

A man of contradictions, Diaghilev was both worldly and superstitious, given to pondering omens and trembling at black cats. A hypochondriac, he would wipe his hands after touching a doorknob—yet he frequently ignored the diabetic's diet prescribed for him by his doctors. He particularly detested sea voyages, for a gypsy fortune-teller once prophesied he would die on the water. And, in a sense, that prophecy came true when he died in Venice in 1929. Not surprisingly, Diaghilev's company died with him. His dancers and choreographers dispersed, but his legacy endured, not simply as a repertoire of great works but as a whole concept of ballet. Diaghilev envisioned ballet as a perfect blending of choreography, dancing, music, and decor, and this desire for total excellence remains a noble—though often prohibitively expen-

To the thousands who flocked to her performances—and to the millions who knew her only by name—Anna Pavlova (opposite) was ballet incarnate. Purists faulted her turn-out, but audiences adored her transcendent artistry, which combined great passion, perfect control, and airy, seemingly effortless dancing. "She made her features speak and her body sing," one critic wrote. And this was true not only of such highly personalized roles as the Dying Swan but of such traditional ones as Giselle and as Princess Aurora in The Sleeping Beauty. *A Bakst costume design for the latter ballet is seen above.*

sive—ideal. Furthermore, through his ambitious productions Diaghilev proved that, far from being a frivolous diversion, as its detractors have alleged, ballet could be serious and eloquent. After Diaghilev, one could still dislike ballet; but one could no longer argue, as many previously had, that it was not a major art.

Though crucially important, Diaghilev's company was not the only worthy ballet company of its day. There was, for example, Les Ballets Suédois, which flourished from 1920 to 1925. Officially Swedish, the company's spiritual home was the Paris art world—hence its French name. With Jean Börlin as choreographer, it modeled itself upon Diaghilev's avant-gardism, commissioning productions from controversial artists. A company of greater fame, however, was the itinerant group directed by Anna Pavlova.

Pavlova—her name is synonymous with "ballerina." The child of a poor family, Pavlova attended the Imperial School of Ballet in St. Petersburg and soon received leading roles at the Maryinsky. She appeared briefly with Diaghilev's company, where she was compared and contrasted with Tamara Karsavina—the former being celebrated for her classical grace, the latter for her dramatic passion. But Pavlova did not really belong with Diaghilev, for their viewpoints were irreconcilably opposed. Diaghilev stressed ballet as a collaborative endeavor, whereas for Pavlova ballet existed to glorify the individual artist. She therefore broke with the Ballets Russes in 1910 and organized her own company. It was a good company, but it had no other female stars, and Pavlova admitted that she liked to hire English girls because they were so docile. Possessed by an almost demonic passion for dancing, Pavlova toured incessantly. Between 1910 and 1925 her company traveled a total of some 300,000 miles and gave nearly 4,000 performances.

Anna Pavlova was one of those great artists who somehow defy all one's usual standards of artistry. For one thing, her taste was dreadfully conventional. Fokine originally planned *Firebird* for her, but when she heard Stravinsky's music she pronounced it nonsense and refused to dance to it. And although she was a notable Giselle, she also adored unabashedly sentimental sketches in which she appeared as a dragonfly or poppy, and she did a coquettish gavotte to the ditty known in English as "The Glow Worm." She also had technical faults, including poor turn-out. Yet she triumphed through the incandescence of her dancing and through her ability to immerse herself totally in whatever she performed. Consequently, what she did wasn't nearly as important as the way in which she did it; she transcended both personal limitations and conventional material.

Pavlova is indelibly associated with *The Dying Swan,* a solo choreographed for her by Fokine. Consisting of a few gliding and fluttering movements, it is almost childishly simple. But Pavlova could reduce grown men and women to tears with it. Her swan had the poignancy of all mortality, and it was her most famous role. Pavlova contracted pneumonia in The Hague in 1931, and as she lay on her deathbed she whispered, "Prepare my swan costume." She died a short time later, and the following night her company played its scheduled performance

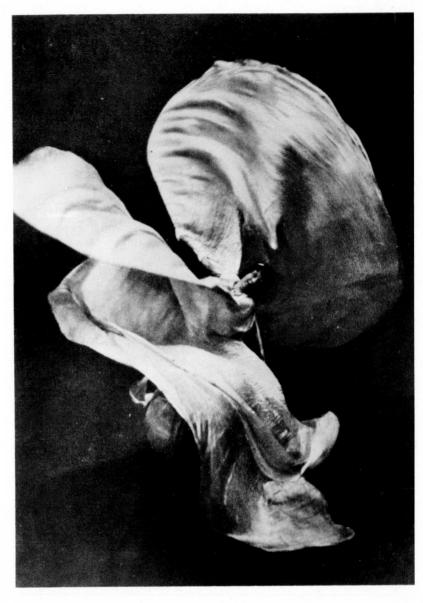

in Brussels. When the time came for *The Dying Swan*, the curtain opened upon an empty stage—and the audience rose in tribute.

However unlike they may have been, both Diaghilev and Pavlova conceived the art of dance as being rooted in classical ballet. His experimentation notwithstanding, Diaghilev admired the classics and in 1921 mounted a complete *Sleeping Beauty*, sumptuously designed by Bakst. Yet even as Diaghilev and Pavlova were revitalizing classicism, revolutionary dancers arose to champion ways of moving that had little or nothing to do with ballet.

Most of these iconoclasts were American. Despite the success of Fanny Elssler, America had not developed a tradition of first-rate ballet, and most of the ballet that did exist was debased and trivial. No wonder, then, that visionary American artists felt compelled to discover their own valid approaches to movement. One such innovator was Loie Fuller, a hardy trouper who began her career as a child prodigy temperance lecturer. She eventually became famous for dances exploiting the effects caused by light falling upon scarfs or veils, the colored light and fluttering draperies creating a lovely shimmer.

Although she fascinated many artists—among them Yeats, who wrote a poem about her—Loie Fuller becomes of secondary importance when compared with Isadora Duncan. Duncan was fond of saying that she first danced in her mother's womb. That statement seems believable enough, for although it is nearly impossible to determine precisely what early training Duncan had, she did dance from childhood on, almost by instinct. In her teens she felt confident enough to march into the office of the theatrical manager Augustin Daly, proclaim herself the spiritual daughter of Walt Whitman, and announce, "I have discovered the dance. I have discovered the art which has been lost for two thousand years."

Whatever he thought of her rhetoric, Daly did give her jobs in shows. But Duncan wanted to present her own dance concerts. Dogged by poverty, she endured the humiliation of dancing in high society drawing rooms and of begging millionaires' wives for money to aid her projects. Thinking she might be better understood abroad, she and her family sailed to Europe on a cattle boat. Gradually, she achieved a reputation—as an eccentric as well as a dancer. Eccentric she certainly was —as were her mother, her sister, and her brothers. Only a starry-eyed family like the Duncans would have attempted to build a palatial residence in their beloved Greece without realizing that there was no water anywhere near their property. And only someone as unpredictable as Isadora—she was known everywhere by her first name—could have advocated socialism while simultaneously praising English servants for their obedience.

But she was more than eccentric. The psychic forces that struggled within her are among those that have shaped the twentieth century. An outspoken feminist, Isadora believed in a woman's right to love and to bear children as she pleased. Torn between liberation and repression, she referred to herself as "a Pagan Puritan, or a Puritanical Pagan," and this awareness helped make her, for all her superficial Hellenism, an essentially American artist, reflecting as it did America's agonized attempts to come to terms with its Puritan heritage. In an era when respectable fathers would say, "I would rather see my daughter dead than on the stage," Isadora dared to dance—and she dreamed of all America dancing with her.

At times, she seemed to live a charmed life; at others, to be plagued by ill fate. After a well-publicized affair with the English actor and designer Gordon Craig, she lived for a time with Paris Singer, whose father had founded the sewing machine company. This idyll was interrupted by a macabre accident that claimed her two children when the car in which they were waiting rolled over an embankment into the Seine. Isadora herself died in an equally strange accident. She had set out with friends for a ride in an open car when the fringe on her shawl caught in the spokes of a wheel. The very first turn of the wheels

Admirers call her the "First Lady of American dance," and not without reason, for Ruth St. Denis devoted half a century to promoting new and uniquely American dance forms. She was applauded in the 1920's for such pseudo-Oriental dances as The Peacock (opposite), but she is admired today as much for her teaching as for her dancing.

broke her neck, killing her instantly. Those present remember that as she stepped into the car, Isadora cried out to her friends, "*Adieu, mes amis. Je vais à la gloire.*"

"I go to glory." Isadora Duncan had attained glory as a prophet of what is called modern dance. Yet her art was so idiosyncratic that it is hard to analyze, although its trappings are obvious enough. The typical Duncan program consisted of dances to classical music performed on a bare stage hung with blue curtains. She wore simple tunics or robes and danced barefoot (which some audiences found as startling as nudity). Her basic movements were confined to walking, running, and skipping. Except for her ambitious use of scores by Beethoven, Wagner, and Gluck, this does not seem like much, yet the effect was apparently tremendous because of her uncanny awareness of dynamics, of movement qualities, and of rhythmic subtleties.

Another modern dance innovator was Isadora's contemporary, Ruth St. Denis. A clue to her personality may reside in the fact that, when young, St. Denis's favorite books were Immanual Kant's *Critique of Pure Reason* and Alexandre Dumas's *Camille*. She was attracted by both metaphysical philosophy and sentimental romance, just as later in life she would be enchanted by mysticism and showbiz. St. Denis's training, like Isadora's, was thoroughly miscellaneous; a bit of ballet, a bit of ballroom dance, a bit of what was known as Delsarte. Delsarte? Let an old song try to explain:

> Every little movement has a meaning all its own,
> Every thought and feeling by some posture may be shown. . . .

This was the hit tune from *Madame Sherry*, a musical comedy of 1910. It spoofs a system of movement study originated by François Delsarte, who attempted to make a scientific examination of the ways emotions and ideas are reflected in posture and gesture. Isadora would have said that he was seeking what she liked to call "key movements"—but without discovering the life force behind them. Indeed, Delsarte's well-meaning but foolish disciples reduced his findings to a set of graceful, insipid poses—the dance equivalent of elocution, the sort of thing suburban clubwomen might do on their lawns in springtime.

Armed with the mastery of some high kicks and a number of statuesque Delsartian poses, the adolescent Ruth St. Denis stormed Broadway. Knowing nothing about agents or managers, she started dancing for the first theatrical employee she saw—a ticket seller. Luckily, the man was kindhearted enough to arrange a proper audition for her. She toured in shows, including several produced by David Belasco, who "canonized" the dancer by changing her name from Dennis to St. Denis. One day, while on tour in Buffalo, she was sipping an ice cream soda in a drugstore when she was galvanized by a poster advertising Egyptian Deities, a brand of cigarettes. Showing the goddess Isis enthroned in a temple, the poster was in no way archaeologically accurate. But it obsessed St. Denis, and it inspired her to go out and create her own kind of dance.

The dance programs she subsequently offered featured works in an Oriental style. The steps were far from authentic, yet the dances were

St. Denis's marriage to dancer-choreographer Ted Shawn in 1914 was marked professionally by a wedding of names. Denishawn, first a school and then a dance company, drew its inspiration and distilled its curriculum from dozens of ethnic sources. St. Denis and Shawn appeared together in works based upon exotic themes, among them "Parvati and the Holy Man" (left, above and below), an item from a suite called East Indian Dances. (Shawn is also seen above in a 1941 revival of St. Denis's Radha.) This remarkable partnership continued until 1932, when the two separated to form their own companies.

lush and lovely, tinged with mysticism. Their sensuality assaulted Victorian drabness in much the same way that Bakst's Oriental designs for Diaghilev had done. In *The Incense*, St. Denis rippled her body as she contemplated burning incense coiling upward; in *The Cobras* she turned her arms into two weaving snakes. As a dancer she was blessed with a beautifully proportioned figure and graceful carriage. Her hair began to go white before she was thirty, but this somehow made her all the more alluring. She was particularly expert in the manipulation of draperies and veils, so that these moving fabrics seemed not mere decorations but magical extensions of her own body.

In 1914 St. Denis met Ted Shawn, who was first her pupil, then her partner, and finally her husband. Shawn, a former divinity student, had taken up dancing as therapy when, as he was recovering from diphtheria, the serum that saved his life temporarily paralyzed him. Together, they organized a company and a wildly eclectic school in Los Angeles called Denishawn. Courses included Oriental, Spanish, and American Indian dances as well as basic ballet—in short, just about any kind of dance St. Denis and Shawn could find. Similarly, the touring Denishawn companies might offer on a single program a Hindu dance, a rhythmic interpretation of concert music, a romantic duet, a hula, and a demonstration of the latest ballroom craze. Such companies could serve as serious cultural attractions and as units on a vaudeville bill, and they even toured as part of the *Ziegfeld Follies*. Branch schools opened around the country and Denishawn survived as an institution until 1932, when its founders went their separate ways, St. Denis to specialize in religious dances and Shawn to organize first an all-male company and then the Jacob's Pillow Dance Festival. In its heyday, Denishawn attracted many talented students, including Martha Graham, Doris Humphrey, and Charles Weidman.

In time, however, these neophytes complained that Denishawn's very eclecticism made it impossible for them to receive more than a casual knowledge of any single dance form. They also insisted that Denishawn too often compromised its ideals in pursuit of commercial success, and that a cult of personality had developed around Shawn and "Miss Ruth," as she was familiarly known. The dancers started walking out; Martha Graham was among the first. Then, at a Denishawn staff meeting in 1928, Doris Humphrey declared that in her opinion Miss Ruth and Shawn cheapened their repertoire when they danced in the *Ziegfeld Follies*. Shawn retorted, "Do you mean to say that Jesus Christ was any the less great because he addressed the common people?" "No," said Humphrey, "but you're not Jesus Christ." To which Shawn responded, "But I am. I am the Jesus Christ of the dance." Shortly thereafter, Humphrey and her partner, Charles Weidman, dropped out of Denishawn.

Across America there existed other choreographic rebels who brought their fervor with them into the studio. Some would build an American ballet; others would create modern dance. The classicists and the moderns were bitter enemies at first, yet they shared the same desire for artistic excellence and, in time, they came to regard each other with respect.

7

The Melting Pot

During the early decades of the twentieth century, Russian hegemony over ballet was nearly complete. The works of Russian choreographers were danced by Russian companies around the world, and the non-Russians who danced with them frequently took Russian names lest they be condemned as second-rate. It is not surprising, then, that America's first ballet companies drew heavily upon Russian émigré talent. Over the years, those companies have become truly international in character, however—and none more so than American Ballet Theatre, featured opposite. Typifying the company's internationalism, California-born Cynthia Gregory and French dancer Michael Denard appear in Unfinished Symphony, *a work by the German-born but French-influenced choreographer Peter van Dyk.*

ONE SUMMER DAY IN 1929 a young American writer named Lincoln Kirstein was sightseeing in Venice. His wanderings eventually brought him to a church, in front of which was moored a black gondola. Inside, a crowd of mourners had gathered. He knew none of them personally, yet they looked oddly familiar, and he therefore lingered for the service. Only sometime later did Kirstein learn that he had unwittingly attended the funeral of Sergei Diaghilev—and that those mourners, so strangely familiar, were Diaghilev's dancers.

Kirstein, whose career was in many ways to parallel Diaghilev's, regarded this incident as an omen. He had been haunted by ballet since his childhood, and he still recollected how bitterly disappointed he had been when his parents decided that their nine-year-old son was too young to attend performances of the Ballets Russes. He finally did see the company in 1924, when he was seventeen—and it was as though he had found the promised land. But Kirstein was not content to be an aficionado of foreign dancers; he dreamed of an American ballet company with its own school, one where dancers could be trained in what would emerge as a distinctively American style. And in 1933 he and a friend named Edward M. M. Warburg set about making the dream a reality. They began by inviting George Balanchine, the choreographer Kirstein most admired, to come to America and head a new school and company. It was a wild scheme, but Balanchine was out of work and jobs were scarce during the Depression years. He therefore accepted the offer, adding that he would love to visit a nation that had produced girls as wonderful as Ginger Rogers. On New Year's Day, 1934, the School of American Ballet opened in a Manhattan studio that had once belonged to Isadora Duncan. The dancers who enrolled there were, by and large, a chubby, ill-assorted lot. Yet all were eager, and Balanchine was eager to start choreographing for them.

At first, Balanchine's new ballets grew by fluke and happenstance. While rehearsing a sequence in which the ensemble ran offstage, for instance, one dancer tripped and fell—and Balanchine kept the incident in the ballet. And when, at another rehearsal, a dancer entered late, that too became part of the choreography. From this emerged *Serenade*, a plotless ballet that is popular today and is considered a notable example of tender lyricism.

When the dancers had learned several works, they presented a New

York season in 1935, calling themselves simply the American Ballet. The repertoire, although limited, was adventuresome, but it failed to find favor with John Martin, the *New York Times* dance critic, who chided the company for its decadent "Riviera aesthetics" and even suggested that it should dismiss Balanchine. Martin, the first full-time dance critic on any American newspaper, was intelligent and devoted, and consequently a denunciation from him was no trivial matter. Eventually, John Martin did come to admire Balanchine, but for Martin in 1935 the American Ballet company was not American enough. A look at several theories and a review of some history may suggest why.

The 1930's—from the Great Depression and New Deal to the outbreak of World War II—were years of intense nationalism. America was in a state of crisis, and its citizens were being urged to join together to achieve national unity. Considerable attention was paid to working-class struggles, to the plight of farmers, and to the growth of labor unions. Ballet, born in the courts of Europe, was seen as a diversion of the aristocracy, those oppressors of the common man. As a result, it was thought to have no place in democratic America, which had, therefore, to create a new dance of its own.

The new dance that these partisans advocated was modern dance, a form that legitimately deserved support. Yet if its proponents were right about modern dance, they were wrong about ballet. Although it arose at court and emphasizes aristocratic dignity of carriage—a virtue that need not be restricted to aristocrats alone—ballet does not inherently reflect any political system. Rather, it somewhat resembles a language. In themselves, English, French, or Italian are neither moral nor immoral, but they can seem to be either when individual speakers employ them for specific purposes. Ballet is similarly flexible: in the seventeenth century, it glorified monarchy; in the twentieth, it has extolled communism. And just as a language can expand by incorporating new words, so ballet expands and revitalizes itself. In its early days it took elements from both elegant court ceremonies and the rough-and-tumble commedia dell'arte. And throughout history choreographers have invented new steps and found fresh uses for the old. Surviving autocracy and adjusting to revolution, ballet has been able to depict princes and peasants, kings and cowboys.

A glance at history shows that the eighteenth century produced at least one great American dancer, John Durang, while at least four appeared in the nineteenth: Mary Ann Lee, Julia Turnbull, Augusta Maywood, and George Washington Smith. Maywood danced successfully at the Paris Opéra, while Smith was famous for his noble style. The roster of foreign celebrities who made American tours includes Fanny Elssler in the nineteenth century and Anna Pavlova, Mikhail Mordkin, and the Diaghilev ballet early in our own. After World War I and the Bolshevik Revolution, many Russian dancers—among them Fokine, Mordkin, and Adolph Bolm—settled in the United States. From 1927–30 Léonide Massine even staged dances for the colossal shows at New York City's Roxy Theater.

That sounds like considerable balletic activity, but consider the record for a moment. It includes the names of many illustrious individuals, but it makes no mention of permanent American ballet companies. The reason for that is simple, of course; there were none, and hence there was little sustained creative development. Standards of training varied alarmingly, with some schools teaching acrobatic tricks to showgirls seeking jobs in Broadway chorus lines. At other schools ignorant teachers threatened children with serious physical injury by putting tiny girls *en pointe* before their feet were sufficiently strong. Needless to say, there were also capable, sensitive teachers who longed for the time when there would be a real American ballet.

Fokine, who organized in New York a technically able company composed of advanced students, never quite adjusted to the New

Write the history of modern American ballet and you inevitably write a biography of George Balanchine. When he began to choreograph for Lincoln Kirstein's struggling, new American Ballet company in 1935, there was very little ballet in America —and so Balanchine created it. For the fledgling troupe's first season he made Serenade *(left), and that plotless lyric ballet is still in the New York City Ballet's repertoire four decades later.*

World. His *Thunderbird*, for instance, was based upon Aztec mythology, but it utilized music by Alexander Borodin and Mikhail Glinka. Bolm apparently responded more positively to the challenges of American life, staging well-received ballets in Chicago. Among these works was *Krazy Kat* (1920), based upon a comic strip of the day. Appointed ballet master of the San Francisco Opera in 1932, he founded the company that survives today as the San Francisco Ballet.

Native-born American choreographers also began to emerge during this period, led by Ruth Page, one of Bolm's pupils who has been active since the 1920's as a choreographer in Chicago. When Willam Christensen took over the San Francisco Ballet in 1937, that company embarked upon a long and fruitful association with the dancing Christensen brothers. Harold Christensen heads the company's school, Lew Christensen succeeded Willam as director in 1955, and Willam went on to establish Ballet West, a Salt Lake City company. In Philadelphia Catherine Littlefield organized the Philadelphia Ballet, which flourished during the 1930's.

After 1932 these pioneering American dance companies suddenly found themselves confronting a formidable rival, a ballet company that prided itself on its Russianness. René Blum and Colonel Wassili de Basil, who formed the Ballets Russes de Monte Carlo in the hope of perpetuating the Diaghilev tradition, brought their company to America for the first time in 1933—and created a sensation. The company's balleri-

Adolph Bolm first toured the United States in 1916 as a member of the Ballets Russes. He returned some years later to choreograph for the Chicago Civic Opera, and in 1933 he moved to San Francisco, where he was to transform the dance ensemble of the San Francisco Opera into a nationally acclaimed company. Since the late 1930's the San Francisco Ballet has been associated with the Christensen brothers. Recent productions include Lew Christensen's Don Juan *(left, below) and a revival of his* Filling Station *(below), a piece of Americana dating from the year 1938.*

nas included the scintillating Alexandra Danilova, but its most publicized stars were three teen-aged prodigies, the "baby ballerinas" Tamara Toumanova, Irina Baronova, and Tatiana Riabouchinska. Audiences adored them, just as movie fans adored such younger child stars as Shirley Temple.

The directors of the new Ballets Russes wished, collectively, to be Diaghilev; perhaps they should have tried to be themselves instead. No one could be a second Diaghilev, as the great director would have been the first to point out. Indeed, Sergei Diaghilev would have snorted to see people copying him, for he stressed innovation rather than nostalgia for past glories. (In this sense, Kirstein's American Ballet company was more truly Diaghilevian in spirit.) Moreover, neither Blum nor de Basil possessed Diaghilev's organizational abilities. Factions, including one headed by Blum himself, were constantly resigning, spite and jealousy abounded, and questions of legal rights to ballets grew increasingly snarled. In eight years, de Basil changed his company's name six times, and by the end of the 1930's he found himself in competition with another Ballet Russe, this one directed by Sergei Denham. Finally, de Basil called his company the Original Ballet Russe, while Denham called his the Ballet Russe de Monte Carlo. The former spent the war in South America, returned to Europe, and then collapsed; the latter toured the United States regularly until its demise in 1963, becoming, in effect if not in name, an American company. All these managerial she-

nanigans could serve as material for farce, if it were not for one tragic footnote: René Blum, brother of French Socialist leader Léon Blum, patron of Proust, and the most cultivated of the Ballet Russe directors, died in a Nazi concentration camp.

Despite their problems, the Ballet Russe troupes produced some important ballets, particularly those choreographed by Massine. The most durable have been *Le Beau Danube* and *Gaîté Parisienne*, two romps in operetta style. The most discussed at the time were Massine's "symphonic ballets." *Choreartium*, for example, was a massive abstraction based on Brahms's Fourth Symphony. Massine's staging of Berlioz's *Symphonie Fantastique*, on the other hand, followed the composer's own scenario about a young man's opium dreams. Other symphonic ballets were allegorical: *Les Présages* (Tchaikovsky's Fifth) depicted the forces that shape man's destiny, while *Seventh Symphony* (Beethoven) concerned myths about the Creation.

George Balanchine has been making new dances and revitalizing familiar classics for fifty years. During that time several generations of dancers have grown from adolescence to maturity under his aegis, and only Balanchine himself (left) has failed to age. He remains a restless, inventive director whose imaginative range seems almost limitless—as such divergent works as Bugaku *(right) and* La Valse *(below, right) suggest.*

Overleaf: *One of the productions of the New York City Ballet's 1972 Stravinsky Festival: Jerome Robbins's* Scherzo Fantastique, *a fusion of color, music, and motion.*

The Ballet Russe tours introduced many Americans to ballet; in doing so, however, they reinforced the notion that ballet was essentially Russian. No wonder, then, that Kirstein's American Ballet was in trouble—for modern dance devotees it was not American enough, for Ballet Russe admirers it was too American. Yet it struggled along into the late 1930's, serving briefly as the resident dance group for the Metropolitan Opera until Balanchine's unconventional choreography shocked the subscribers. Happily, the choreographer who unsettled the dowagers of the grand tier wowed Broadway and Hollywood, and the dance sequences that Balanchine composed for such musicals as *On Your Toes* (with its "Slaughter on Tenth Avenue" gangster ballet), *Babes in Arms*, and *The Boys from Syracuse*—and for such films as *The Goldwyn Follies*—were enormously popular.

To give his dancers additional employment and to encourage young

choreographers, Kirstein in 1936 formed a second company, Ballet Caravan. As such titles as *Pocahontas* and *Yankee Clipper* suggest, the repertoire featured American themes. Americana became extremely popular in the late 1930's and early 1940's, as choreographers sought to prove that ballet was fully capable of treating American subject matter. Two works typify Ballet Caravan's Americana. Lew Christensen's *Filling Station*, set to Virgil Thomson's music, offers a cartoonlike portrait of the American highway, its characters including a filling station attendant, his truck driver friends, some passing motorists, and a gangster pursued by state troopers. Eugene Loring's *Billy the Kid*, with its Aaron Copland score, juxtaposes scenes from the life of the outlaw with panoramic representations of the settling of the West.

World War II brought both the American Ballet and Ballet Caravan companies to an end. When peace came, Kirstein and Balanchine embarked upon a new venture, Ballet Society, a noncommercial organization founded in 1946 to present experimental works for a limited subscription audience. In 1948 the new company gave a series of performances at the New York City Center of Music and Drama, an auditorium the city had acquired in 1943. These performances so impressed Morton Baum, chairman of the City Center finance committee, that he offered to make Ballet Society an official part of City Center. Kirstein, struck speechless for a moment, finally responded: "If you do that for us, I will give you in three years the finest ballet company in America."

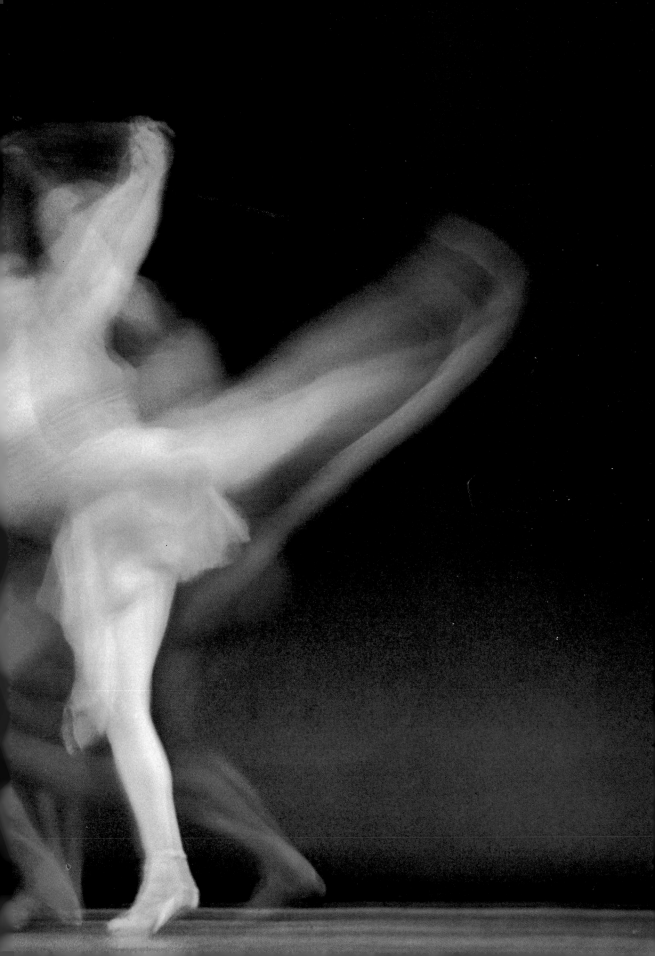

Kirstein kept his promise, and under his aegis the New York City Ballet, as Ballet Society was renamed, became one of the world's greatest dance companies. Although many talented choreographers have collaborated with the company over the years, its repertoire is dominated by Balanchine and it is Balanchine who has given the company its distinctive image. A prolific, imperturbable worker, Balanchine has been producing ballets for decades in a ceaseless flow of invention. Even-tempered, he seldom sulks and rarely rages. He likes to say that his muse comes to him "on union time," and he describes choreography not as a grandiose intellectual endeavor but as a skill akin to cooking.

Balanchine's ballets range from a serene retelling of the Orpheus myth to an adaptation of *A Midsummer Night's Dream* to such works as *La Sonnambula*, a macabre story about a sleepwalker that is the kind of thing Edgar Allan Poe might have concocted had he been a choreographer. His most distinctive pieces, however, are his plotless or abstract ballets. He was not the inventor of the abstract ballet—Fokine holds that distinction with *Les Sylphides*—but no choreographer has worked so extensively in this genre. His narrative ballets notwithstanding, Balanchine is essentially an antiliterary choreographer. "Why should we do Shakespeare?" he once commented. "Shakespeare's already done Shakespeare." Only what can be revealed through movement interests Balanchine, and he has removed from many ballets not only plot but even elaborate costumes and scenery, so that nothing will distract attention from the movement itself. Balanchine puts his faith in the power and beauty of movement, and his faith is deep.

Balanchine's best works combine extraordinary technical flexibility and a profound reverence for the inflexible canons of classical ballet. The former quality is especially evident in such works as Movements for Piano and Orchestra *(above), which perfectly reflects the dissonances of its Stravinsky score. (Allegra Kent and Jacques d'Amboise stand at right in the photograph.) The latter is on display in* Jewels, *a magnificently mounted three-act plotless ballet (right, featuring Kay Mazzo and Peter Martins in the "Diamonds" sequence).*

The movement he devises for an abstract composition is prompted by its score, but his ballets are not music appreciation lessons. Balanchine does not attempt to match each separate note or instrument with a gesture; rather, the music's moods and rhythms are reflected in the scale and sweep of the dance. The rigor of Bach's Concerto for Two Violins resulted in the crisp, bracing *Concerto Barocco*, for instance. In contrast, Tchaikovsky's lush Second Piano Concerto led Balanchine to produce *Ballet Imperial*, an opulent work in the Petipa style.

Dancegoers unfamiliar with Balanchine need not feel intimidated by the word "abstract"—for one does not need to master erudite theories to understand Balanchine; all one has to do is to watch closely as the choreography unfolds. Although there are few stories in Balanchine's ballets, the ways dancers move in space frequently evoke moods or emotional relationships. The movement may be agitated or relaxed, carefree or somber, graceful or slashing; the manner in which dancers touch or separate may suggest attraction or revulsion, desire or indifference. Events crystallize like designs in a kaleidoscope, and the sum total of these events gives each ballet its particular flavor. *The Four Temperaments* (Hindemith), for example, is as enigmatic as the symbols of a medieval alchemist. One episode of *Scotch Symphony* (Mendelssohn), on the other hand, presents a woman as ethereal and unattainable as any sylphide. *Liebeslieder Walzer* (Brahms) simply shows couples waltzing in a ballroom, but in their waltzing are innumerable hints of flirtation, courtship, infatuation, and mature worldly wisdom.

Balanchine's basic vocabulary of movement is classical ballet as inherited from Petipa. Yet when using contemporary music, he often distorts academic classicism with odd shifts of weight or energy—not merely for shock effect but to build a whole new and refreshing structure out of familiar steps, just as an inventive poet can construct unexpected images out of simple words. Among modern composers, Balanchine has particularly respected Stravinsky, and until his death in 1971 Stravinsky found Balanchine an unusually sympathetic choreographic collaborator. The most famous Balanchine-Stravinsky ballet is probably *Agon*. Its title is the Greek word for "contest," and the work could be described as a set of games or athletic events. But the choreography's rhythmic thrust is so quick and biting and the atmosphere is so electric that the episodes seem like Olympian games for young gods. *Agon* is sometimes considered one of three Balanchine-Stravinsky works deriving from Greek sources, the others being *Apollo* and *Orpheus*. Each celebrates the civilizing power of art, *Apollo* and *Orpheus* expressing the idea in terms of Greek mythology, *Agon* doing so abstractly.

Like Picasso, Balanchine has shown that a work may be nonrepresentational and still possess profound significance. In so doing he has extended the range of his art—an achievement that may qualify him for the honor of being America's finest ballet choreographer. Americanism in ballet is more than a matter of picking local subjects, although Balanchine has done that, creating works to Sousa marches (*Stars and Stripes*) and Gershwin songs (*Who Cares?*). Responding to America's fundamental vigor and physicality—and to the freshness of American people at their best—Balanchine has produced ballets that are swift, athletic, and frank. Their language is classical; their accent, American.

After the New York City Ballet, the country's leading company is American Ballet Theatre, founded in 1939 as Ballet Theatre. Its nucleus was the Mordkin Ballet, a group directed by Mikhail Mordkin that performed classics and works in a traditional Russian style. But Ballet Theatre's first director, Richard Pleasant, had bolder ambitions. He envisioned a diversified company that could preserve and exhibit examples of many styles and periods. Consequently, for Ballet Theatre's initial season Pleasant assembled works by eleven choreographers—ranging from such masters as Fokine and Nijinska to comparative unknowns. After Pleasant entered military service in World War II the company was run by several directors and managers. Then, in 1945, Lucia Chase and Oliver Smith were appointed co-directors, positions they still hold. As a wealthy young widow, Chase had become intensely interested in dance, and she had appeared in leading roles with the Mordkin Ballet. She provided much of the financial backing for Ballet Theatre's first season, and she has unstintingly contributed to the company ever since. Entering the field a rich amateur, she has become a thorough professional, single-minded in her devotion to ballet.

Over the years, Chase and Smith have tried to remain true to the catholic spirit of Richard Pleasant's original concept. American Ballet Theatre has staged such classics as *Swan Lake*, *Giselle*, *Coppélia*, *La Sylphide*, *Les Sylphides*, *Petrouchka*, and excerpts from *Napoli*; it has commissioned new ballets and has revived modern works first produced by other companies. Loring's *Billy the Kid*, created for Ballet Caravan,

When American Ballet Theatre opened its second New York season in 1941, it did so with the startling announcement that henceforth its roster would recognize only "principal dancers" and "members of the company." Later the company did return to a more traditional ranking system, but its choreographic range has always remained eclectic. In addition to successful revivals of Giselle *(above, with Alicia Alonso) and* Swan Lake *(opposite, with Natalia Makarova and Ivan Nagy), the company was to produce such contemporary works as Eugene Loring's* Billy the Kid *(below, with John Kriza and Lupe Serrano).*

is now a Ballet Theatre favorite, as is Agnes de Mille's *Rodeo*, commissioned by the Ballet Russe de Monte Carlo in 1942.

The year 1942 is a significant one in the history of American dance, for *Rodeo's* production was a sign that the Ballet Russe, separated by war from Europe, was willing to drop some of its foreign affectations and declare itself an American company. *Rodeo*, set to Aaron Copland music, is the story of a tomboyish cowgirl who realizes that in order to compete with frilly girls for the attention of the ranch hands she too

Although A.B.T. actively encouraged the creation of truly American ballets by native-born choreographers, it was the Ballet Russe de Monte Carlo that first staged Agnes de Mille's Rodeo. *Initially, de Mille herself (left) danced the role of the hoyendish heroine—and by the time she had passed on to other things her exuberant ballet had passed into A.B.T.'s repertoire. That assemblage now includes such disparate works as de Mille's* Fall River Legend *and Jerome Robbins's* Fancy Free. *Eliot Feld, who danced in a revival of the latter work, was later to produce a number of dances for A.B.T., among them* Theatre *(opposite), before departing to form his own company.*

has to dress in a ladylike fashion. An ingenious technical device used in *Rodeo* and Loring's *Billy the Kid* is a spread-legged, bent-kneed stance. It not only makes the dancers resemble bowlegged cowboys, but can even foster the illusion that they are riding horses across the stage.

Agnes de Mille, granddaughter of economist Henry George, daughter of writer-director William C. de Mille, and niece of movie potentate Cecil B. de Mille, has been particularly interested in the introduction of ordinary American gesture into ballet. One of her best-known

pieces for Ballet Theatre is *Fall River Legend*, freely based upon the legend of Lizzie Borden. De Mille has also choreographed such musical comedy hits as *Oklahoma!*, *Bloomer Girl*, and *Brigadoon*.

Of all choreographers introduced to America by Ballet Theatre, the most important has been British-born Antony Tudor, who was a clerk in London's Smithfield Market until performances by the Pavlova and Diaghilev companies made him enamored of dancing. He began by taking ballet lessons and soon shifted to choreography, creating such works as *The Planets*, *The Descent of Hebe*, and his first masterpieces, *Jardin aux Lilas* and *Dark Elegies*. A New York resident since Ballet Theatre's first season, he has revived productions originally staged in London and has created new works.

Like Balanchine, Tudor extends the range of ballet—but in a totally different direction. Whereas Balanchine glories in movement as a self-sufficient entity, Tudor uses movement to reveal psychological states. He looks inward and, through movement, makes thought and feeling visible, thereby giving new depth and profundity to narrative ballet. Tudor's ballets—and there are not many, for he is a painstaking choreographer—employ the classical vocabulary, but sequences of traditional steps are distorted or broken to suggest the changes of a character's mind and the way he may be pulled by conflicting desires or by regrets and yearnings. Under such circumstances, small gestures can be as important as large leaps. The wave of a hand or the flick of a wrist can reveal volumes about a character, and such gestures flow by like pangs, sighs, or passing fancies.

Tudor's ballets frequently combine psychological insight with social comment. *Jardin aux Lilas* concerns a woman about to be wed, in a marriage of convenience, to a man she does not love. At a party in her honor she encounters both her own lover and her fiancé's former mistress. The ballet is a constant series of interruptions, of furtive meetings

and hasty partings, the characters concealing their anguish behind a mask of upper-class manners. The final irony of the situation is that, though all these people are well-to-do, their money and social positions actually hinder rather than aid them in their search for personal happiness. Also contrasting desire and repression, *Pillar of Fire* reveals the torment of a shy woman who, fearing spinsterhood and wrongly suspecting that the man for whom she feels affection is indifferent to her, commits what her straitlaced community would call a moral indiscretion. Other Tudor ballets include *Undertow*, which traces the events that lead a man to commit a sex crime; *Dark Elegies*, a ritual of bereavement; and *Romeo and Juliet*, a choreographic meditation upon

The intense, introspective ballets of English choreographer Antony Tudor (below, left) have been a feature of A.B.T.'s repertory season after season. One of the earliest and most powerful of these dances is Dark Elegies *(above, left) set to Gustav Mahler's melancholy Kindertotenlieder. The ballets of Jerome Robbins (right) also have strong psychological overtones. His version of* Afternoon of a Faun *(above, with Jacques D'Amboise and Kay Mazzo) is widely interpreted as a commentary on the innate narcissism of all dancers.*

Overleaf: One of America's best-known small companies, the Joffrey Ballet, set out on its first tour in a single rented station wagon. Today it is a resident company of New York City Center, where it presents a varied repertoire and conducts an exemplary apprentice program.

the themes of Shakespeare's play. If Balanchine emphasizes the extroversion of American dancers, Tudor—our other great émigré choreographer—is involved with the expression of intense personal feeling. Together, they have profoundly influenced American ballet style.

The same must be said for New York-born Jerome Robbins, whose first work, *Fancy Free*, to a score by the young Leonard Bernstein, was given its premiere by Ballet Theatre in 1944. Its plot was simple—three sailors on shore leave during World War II try to pick up some girls —but its spirit was so rambunctious that it became a repertoire staple. Its seemingly artless fun results from meticulous craftsmanship, for Robbins has fused ballet, Broadway, jazz, Harlem, and Hollywood dance styles of the 1940's in such a way that, looking upon it now, this 1944 comedy seems as much of an authentic period piece as a ballet from 1844 would be.

Fancy Free's robust use of nonclassical and popular idioms is typical of Robbins. Working for both American Ballet Theatre and New York

City Ballet, he has been most eclectic. His *Interplay* is a bouncy jazz suite; *Afternoon of a Faun* reinterprets Nijinsky's old ballet, transforming the Faun into a narcissistic dancer; *Moves* is a ballet in silence that looks abstract yet manages to suggest countless emotional complications. *The Cage*, premiered in 1951, created a scandal because Robbins intimated that the way certain predatory female insects, such as the mantis, devour their partners after mating might have parallels in human sexual relationships. His basic theatricality has made Robbins a vigorous choreographer and director on Broadway, where his successes include *West Side Story*, *Gypsy*, and *Fiddler on the Roof*. Robbins's recent productions for the New York City Ballet have been unusually varied. *Dances at a Gathering* and *Goldberg Variations*, both of them suites of witty and lyrical episodes set to Chopin and Bach, respectively, suggest implicit faith in human goodness, while *In the Night*, also to Chopin, examines the romantic relationships of three couples. *Watermill*, a controversial, allegorical account of a man's life from youth to old age, is performed in hypnotic slow motion.

Robbins's willingness to explore divergent dance forms seems an instance of American pragmatism. It is a trait shared by Eliot Feld, whose choreographic debut, *Harbinger*, was presented by American Ballet Theatre in 1967. He has since produced ballets for various groups, among them the Joffrey and Royal Winnipeg ballets. Some of these works betray the influences of Robbins, Balanchine, and Tudor—but these are all worthy people to be influenced by, and Feld also possesses a brashness and sensitivity all his own.

In addition to the large ballet companies, there are several important smaller troupes. Robert Joffrey founded one of these in 1956 when he and a few dancers rented a station wagon and embarked upon a tour of one-night stands. Despite financial hardship, Joffrey persisted—and today the City Center Joffrey Ballet is a thriving adjunct to the New York City Center. Over the years, Joffrey's company has exhibited an intriguing split personality. On the one hand, it cultivates a pop image with such ostentatiously hip rock-ballets as Gerald Arpino's *Trinity* and *Sacred Grove on Mount Tamalpais* and Joffrey's *Astarte*, a mixed-media spectacular that combines live dancers with films and psychedelic lighting effects. But the repertoire also offers a representative sampling of works by Bournonville, Fokine, Massine, Balanchine, and Robbins, as well as *The Green Table*, by the German expressionist choreographer Kurt Jooss, an antiwar ballet that satirizes the hypocrisy of diplomats and presents grim battlefield vignettes. It dates from 1932 and was obviously inspired by World War I; unfortunately for the political state of the world, it remains naggingly topical.

At the turn of the century, the United States was a balletic backwater. Now it is, along with England and Russia, one of the "big three" nations of the ballet world and the one in which ballet activities are the most diversified. During its great waves of immigration, America was called a melting pot of nationalities. That metaphor also applies to contemporary American ballet, which is the result of many artistic influences. All the companies mentioned have made their contribution—as have many others. The art patron Rebekah Harkness has sponsored

Abandoning a highly successful career as a soloist with George Balanchine's New York City Ballet, Arthur Mitchell (seen above) founded a pioneering all-black ballet company in 1971. Dance Theatre of Harlem, as Mitchell's group is known, presents works like Milko Sparemblek's Ancient Voices of Children, *seen at right.*

several companies bearing the name of the Harkness Ballet, and these groups have toured America and Europe. Arthur Mitchell, a black dancer and former member of the New York City Ballet, directs Dance Theatre of Harlem, a ballet-based group.

Outside New York, thriving professional companies include the sprightly Boston Ballet, the Cincinnati Ballet, the Pennsylvania Ballet of Philadelphia, the San Francisco Ballet, and Salt Lake City's Ballet West. There are also dozens of semiprofessional and nonprofessional companies throughout the country, offering young dancers valuable training experience. Many are affiliated with the National Association for Regional Ballet, an organization dedicated to the improvement of dance at the grass-roots level.

In American ballet one can expect the unexpected. In 1973, for instance, Twyla Tharp staged two works for the Joffrey Ballet. Tharp is a modern dancer with a reputation for almost mathematically complex abstract choreography. Her Joffrey creations were *Deuce Coupe*, danced to Beach Boys tunes against a backdrop inspired by New York City subway-car graffiti, and *As Time Goes By*, set to a Haydn symphony. Balletgoers were charmed by both, for ballet is increasingly developing friendly relations with another way of dancing—the modern dance. A product of our century and therefore only a lusty youngster compared to ballet, modern dance has nevertheless managed to lead quite a tumultuous life.

8

Dance in Ferment

For half a century dancers and dance critics alike have sought and failed to find a suitable substitute for the term "modern dance." The first dances made by Martha Graham scarcely seem modern today, and yet they herald works like Alvin Ailey's indisputably modern Revelations *(opposite). Whatever these dances are, they clearly are not classical ballet. They belong instead to that most eclectic of dance forms—modern dance—where, in the words of an early proponent of the form, "There are no general rules."*

AFTER MARTHA GRAHAM'S DEBUT CONCERT in 1926 a bewildered acquaintance exclaimed, "It's dreadful! Martha, how long do you expect to keep this up?" Graham replied, "As long as I have an audience." Many other theatergoers experienced similar bewilderment in the early days of modern dance, but their confusion did not deter the dancers, whose persistence eventually gained them a wide and highly enthusiastic audience.

The term "modern dance" has never pleased anyone—critics, choreographers, or dance historians. It has stuck, however, and a better name has yet to be found. Nor has anyone managed to invent a concise definition of just what modern dance is, although the historian, pressed for a description, might say that modern dance is a form of Western theatrical dancing that has developed almost entirely outside the ballet tradition. Its spiritual ancestors are Isadora Duncan, Ruth St. Denis, and Ted Shawn, but its pioneers include dancers who rebelled against Denishawn's artistic limitations, just as St. Denis and Shawn had rebelled against the limitations of an earlier era of dance.

Modern dance is not simply a matter of chronology, however, nor is it a rigid technical system. In essence, it is a point of view that stresses artistic individualism and encourages dancers to develop personal choreographic styles. According to this philosophy, there are as many valid ways of dancing as there are skillful choreographers—an outlook that was cogently expressed in 1927 in program notes for a concert by Helen Tamiris: "There are no general rules. Each work of art creates its own code."

The early days of modern dance—the 1920's and 1930's—were days of adventure. Despite the Great Depression and the bewilderment of audiences, choreographers proceeded undaunted. They virtually reinvented dance as they went along, a process that began with the rejection of ballet, which they considered hidebound and trivial. It is perhaps significant that the two nations in which modern dance took strongest hold, America and Germany, were nations that had no celebrated ballet companies, a situation that led ambitious dancers to experiment with new forms. Their iconoclasm occasionally went to grim extremes, however. Because ballet movements were by and large rounded and symmetrical, for example, modern dancers emphasized angular asymmetries. The result was that early modern dance tended to be fierce; it hugged the ground and was resolutely unglamorous. Its exponents disdained frills, preferring to look sturdy and earthy rather than conform to stereotyped ideals of grace.

Save for Harald Kreutzberg in Germany and Ted Shawn and Charles Weidman in America, most modern dance pioneers were women. A public that branded male dancers effeminate—and thereby discouraged many potentially great dancers from entering the field— tolerated female dancers, even while suspecting their virtue. Modern dance gave women an opportunity to proclaim their independence from conventionality, both as artists and as women, and many seized the opportunity.

In general, the moderns focused upon the expressive powers of movement. So, of course, did Isadora Duncan and the Diaghilev choreographers. But whereas Isadora and Diaghilev combined movement with fine music—and, in Diaghilev's case, with fine art—in order to prove that movement could hold its own with the other two, the early moderns minimized the other arts. Music was frequently composed after a dance had been choreographed and it sometimes consisted only of percussion rhythms. Costumes were spartan, and as a result wags have called this the "long woolens" period of modern dance.

Modern dance developed independently in America and Germany, thriving in the former locale but fading in the latter in the wake of the Nazi holocaust. Before World War II, the greatest exponent of German modern dance was Mary Wigman, who had been a student of Emile Jaques-Dalcroze, inventor of a system designed to foster a sense of musical rhythm, and of Rudolf von Laban, who tried to apply scientific principles to movement analysis. Despite her teachers' intellectuality, Wigman's art appealed to the instincts. A stocky, muscular woman who fitted no one's idea of prettiness, Wigman created sombre,

macabre, almost demonic dances that hinted at the primitive drives still lurking beneath the veneer of civilization. Wigman felt she was in contact with primordial forces that took possession of her as she performed, and she often wore masks in order to escape her ordinary personality and yield herself to these powers. So awesome were these forces on occasion that Wigman, convinced that the mask represented a spirit attempting to consume her utterly, became terrified by her own choreography.

Wigman toured America in the 1930's, and shortly thereafter she sent one of her assistants, Hanya Holm, to open a New York branch of the Wigman school. After a few years Holm realized that American bodies and temperaments were so markedly different from those she had

Americans have so thoroughly dominated modern dance almost from its inception that the major contributions made by such innovative early German choreographers as Harald Kreutzberg (above, left) and Mary Wigman are frequently overlooked. In some German works the dancers accompanied themselves on percussion instruments (below, left) as they moved. Among native innovators, Martha Graham is recognized as "the senior star and greatest exponent of the American modern dance." Ted Shawn choreographed her first solo—that of an Aztec princess in Xochitl *(above)—in 1919, but since 1926 Graham has choreographed her own works. At right is* Celebration, *a 1934 group piece based upon exuberant jumping patterns.*

encountered in Germany that she could not replicate Wigman's style. She therefore asked for and received permission to rename the school the Hanya Holm Studio and to run it as an independent institution. Over the ensuing years Holm has choreographed for her own company and has set the dances for such well-known musicals as *Kiss Me, Kate* and *My Fair Lady*.

Of American modern dancers, the most famous is surely Martha Graham. Indeed, to many people her name is virtually synonymous with modern dance. She once said that she views each of her works as "a graph of the heart," a statement that reveals much about her art. Equally significant is the fact that when she was a little girl her father, a physician specializing in nervous disorders, warned her never to lie because he would always know when she was lying by the tensions in her body. She remembered that warning, and in her dances she has tried to tell the truth, however unpleasant it may be. Graham can be equally strong-willed offstage; as a young woman, she disconcerted friends by her tendency, when aroused, to bare her teeth like a shark.

Like that other artistic experimentalist, Gertrude Stein, Graham was born in Allegheny, Pennsylvania. Able to trace her ancestry back to

Miles Standish, Graham grew up in an atmosphere of Presbyterian rectitude. When her family moved to Santa Barbara because of her sister's asthma, Graham found herself in a less stern environment—and it was in California that she first saw Ruth St. Denis perform. She knew then that she wanted to dance, but she did not dare enroll in the Denishawn school until after her father's death. The force of family tradition had battled against her personal desires, a conflict that would be reflected in her choreography.

After some years with Denishawn, Graham was encouraged to go her own choreographic way by Louis Horst, who was Denishawn's conductor at the time. (Later Horst was to serve as accompanist and father confessor to the whole early generation of American modern dancers.) Graham started choreographing programs in which Denishawn exoticism gave way to a strident angularity that caused some observers to compare her to a cube. She also started teaching, taking in a young actress named Bette Davis as one of her early pupils. Among other things, Graham taught Davis to fall down a flight of stairs without injury—it was such a spectacular stunt that Davis got one role on the basis of that trick alone.

Like many modern dancers, past and present, Graham invented her technique as she went along. The kinds of movements she and her company practiced were based upon whatever creative problems were troubling her. Early Graham technique was notorious for its nervous jerks and tremblings. Yet it was by no means irrational, for she based it upon a fundamental fact of life: breathing. Graham studied the bodily changes that occur during inhalation and exhalation, and from her observations developed the principles known as contraction and release. She then experimented with the dynamics of the process, allowing contractions to possess whiplash intensity. Unlike classical ballet, which typically tried to conceal effort, Graham sought to reveal it because she believed that life itself was effort. Eventually her technique incorporated softer, more lyrical, elements, but it never ceased to be a vehicle for passion. Her productions also grew richer in terms of music and scenery, many being collaborations with sculptor Isamu Noguchi.

Graham's percussive style enabled her to express emotional extremes. Some of her dances, to the dismay of rationalists, resembled visions of medieval mystics, who could combine flagellation with exaltation. Graham's finest early achievement in this vein is *Primitive Mysteries*, a 1931 work based upon the rites of Christianized Indians in the American Southwest that features a cult of female worshipers trying to emulate the Virgin Mary, sinking into dolor at the Crucifixion and rejoicing at the Resurrection.

After the Depression, many choreographers turned to themes of social protest. Graham, who seldom chose overtly topical themes, did choose during the course of the next decade to examine the forces that helped shape American society. *Frontier* (1935) offered a portrait of a pioneer woman facing the vastness of the American continent, at first with trepidation but ultimately with confidence. *Act of Judgment* attacked the crippling influence of Puritanism, a theme to which Graham returned with *Letter to the World*, in which the New Eng-

Graham has survived all her early critics, and in so doing she has risen above criticism. Those who found her first offerings opaque, mystifying, and graceless are gone; those who remain are spellbound by the power of her more recent dance dramas derived from history, legend, and Greek mythology. At right she dances her 1951 solo, The Triumph of St. Joan, *which she later expanded into the group dance* Seraphic Dialogue.

121

land poet Emily Dickinson is thwarted by Puritan repression as personified by a terrifying dowager called the Ancestress. In *Appalachian Spring* (1944), a fire-and-brimstone revivalist preacher thunders at a housewarming for a newly married couple. But the newlyweds' love for each other and the common sense of a pioneer woman triumph over Calvinism. With this resolution Graham apparently made peace with her heritage, for she has never taken up the theme again. Over the years, Graham has repeatedly commissioned works by contemporary composers, the music Aaron Copland provided for *Appalachian Spring* being possibly the best single score of her career.

Since the 1940's, Graham has largely concerned herself with dance dramas depicting figures from history, literature, and mythology. She uses these characters as embodiments of psychological traits that are universal to mankind. *Errand into the Maze*, for instance, derives from the myth of Theseus and the Minotaur but does not literally tell that

To Doris Humphrey, all of dance existed on "the arc between two deaths," the area of movement between absolute motionlessness and complete collapse. Her works therefore stressed the dynamics of balance and imbalance, extension, fall, and recovery (shown in the photographs above and at left).

story. Rather, it shows a woman shuddering her way through a labyrinth, where she confronts a creature—half man, half beast—who personifies her own fears. *Deaths and Entrances*, suggested by the life of the Brontë sisters, mingles fancy and fact as three sisters handle objects in their house (a vase, a shell, a chesspiece) that trigger memories.

Graham's dances often begin at a climactic moment in the protagonist's life, with the heroine—for they are usually about women—recalling past events as she moves toward her destiny. This retrospective approach is most elaborately developed in the evening-long *Clytemnestra*, in which the ancient Greek queen, condemned to Hades, reflects upon her murderous past and slowly comes to terms with herself. Another favorite Graham device is to divide a character into different facets and have each personified by a separate dancer, as in *Seraphic Dialogue*, in which the spirit of Joan of Arc contemplates herself as maiden, warrior, and martyr.

Throughout her career, Graham has prompted adulation and controversy. Some have faulted her for obscurity, others for obviousness; occasionally her work has been called obscene. Yet she continues to choreograph, and no matter how much her style changes, her works share one common quality—total commitment.

Graham was not the only influential early modern dancer. The list also includes Helen Tamiris, for instance. She was born Helen Becker, but changed her name when she found a poem about a Persian queen that contained the line "Thou art Tamiris, the ruthless queen who banishes all obstacles." At a time when many modern dancers favored a gaunt look, Tamiris was flamboyant and something of a hellion. Fascinated by the American past, she choreographed dances to Whitman poems, Revolutionary War songs, and Louisiana bayou ballads. Her *Negro Spirituals* was one of the first works choreographed by a white to take black culture seriously. As adept on Broadway as she was on the concert stage, Tamiris also choreographed several musicals, including *Up in Central Park* and *Annie Get Your Gun*.

If Graham had a real rival for choreographic eminence, however, it was Doris Humphrey, who grew up in the Chicago area where her parents managed a hotel that had a theatrical clientele. She took ballet lessons as a girl and, as often happened in a period when standards of dance training varied considerably, studied with both eminent masters and unbalanced eccentrics. The latter ranged from a Viennese lady who claimed that a diet of gooseberries promoted bodily agility to a gentleman who pinched little Doris as she went through her exercises. Humphrey joined Denishawn in 1917, only to rebel against that method eleven years later. She and her partner, Charles Weidman, thereupon established their own group. Weidman became famous for his deft pantomime, his compositions spoofing silent films, and his mimetic studies inspired by James Thurber. Humphrey, for her part, had more cosmic ambitions. Like Graham, she forged a technique from elementary principles of movement. But whereas Graham had emphasized breathing, Humphrey concentrated upon balance, her key words being "fall" and "recovery."

Humphrey's choreography was based upon the muscular drama of

balance and imbalance, the contrasts between giving way to gravity altogether and resisting gravity to regain equilibrium. Conflict is inherent in such movement, and many Humphrey works were monumental explorations of human conflict. *The Shakers* (1931) examined the customs of a nineteenth-century celibate sect that believed one could rid oneself of sin by literally shaking it out of the body. Humphrey's dance, in depicting this process of shaking, hinted that sexual repression was an unacknowledged source of the devotees' frenzy. During 1935 and 1936 Humphrey choreographed the *New Dance* trilogy, her most ambitious treatment of conflict and resolution. The first section, *Theatre Piece*, satirized the rat race of competitive society. *With My Red Fires*, the second piece, castigated possessive love as personified by a matriarchal figure who thwarts her daughter's romantic desires. Having chastised communal and personal failings, Humphrey finally attempted to visualize an ideal social order in which the individual and the group could exist in accord. This finale, called simply *New Dance*, was entirely abstract in form.

Modern dance's stress upon creativity encouraged dancers to go out and organize new companies. Just as Graham and Humphrey left Denishawn, so fledglings started leaving Graham and Humphrey-Weidman. Anna Sokolow, for example, left Graham in 1938 and later created

Mexican-born José Limón came to New York to study art, but after attending a single dance performance he enrolled instead in a school run by Humphrey and her partner, Charles Weidman. In time Limón was to form a company of his own and—with Humphrey serving as artistic advisor—produce such classics of modern dance as Missa Brevis, There Is a Time, and The Moor's Pavane (above), which Limón danced with Betty Jones. A brass band provided the music for Paul Taylor's 1954 debut and marked his company as one of the nation's most inventive. American Genesis (above, right), for example, deals with Old Testament parables in a nineteenth-century American setting. Here, Noah's children put on a minstrel show.

works, set to jazz scores, about the loneliness and alienation of life in big cities. A Humphrey-Weidman dancer who headed an unusually successful troupe was José Limón. His declaration of independence from Humphrey-Weidman was accomplished without rancor, and until her death Humphrey served as Limón's artistic advisor. The Mexican-born Limón, with his deep-set eyes and hollow cheeks, possessed a brooding presence that suggested an Indian heritage. His dances tended to be strongly dramatic, and his heroes were saints, sinners on a grand scale, and holy fools. Limón's most durable composition has been *The Moor's Pavane* (1949), an adaptation of *Othello* that sustains tension by placing the machinations of Iago and the jealousy of Othello within the strict decorum of old court dances. Maintaining surface politeness, the characters dance out a pavane that finally explodes into catastrophe.

By the 1950's, modern dance was recognized as an authentic American art. Lamentably, some of its original energy had been drained away over the years, a factor that led disenchanted younger choreographers to declare that modern dance was so oriented toward drama and narrative that it had become a form of pantomime and had lost sight of movement as something beautiful and fascinating for its own sake. The new choreographers advocated a dance that was abstract, nonliteral, and evocative rather than explicit.

Erick Hawkins, Graham's former husband, proclaimed what he called "movement quality" to be the essence of all dancing. The qualities he seemed most fond of were softness, gentleness, and ceremoniousness—attributes that give his work an almost Oriental serenity. Paul Taylor, on the other hand, is a dancer with a strong, heavy body who can nonetheless move with wit and grace—and those qualities abound in his choreography. His compositions include *Aureole*, a lyric dance that has a balletic feeling although its actual steps would astonish Petipa; *Orbs*, a meditation upon the seasons of the year, set to Beethoven quartets; and *American Genesis*, which gives familiar Bible stories American settings, turning Cain and Abel into feuding cowboys, Noah's ark into a Mississippi riverboat, and the Creation itself into the landing of the Pilgrims. Taylor is aware of human frailty but, unlike some of the dramatic choreographers of the 1940's who wrapped themselves in the gloom of Freudian dogma, he makes his social comments with an unmistakable twinkle in his eye.

Alwin Nikolais boasts that he is an artistic polygamist. What he seeks, he says, is "a polygamy of motion, shape, color, and sound." A complete man of the theater, Nikolais choreographs the dances, composes the electronic music, and designs the scenery, costumes, and lighting for all his productions, which are abstract mixed-media pieces of dazzling complexity. These pieces, surprising as conjuring tricks, could be regarded as contemporary equivalents of the masques and spectacles that delighted monarchs back in the seventeenth century. But if the old masques glorified monarchy, Nikolais's spectacles extol the wonders of the electronic age. He likes to transform dancers by encasing them in fantastic costumes or by attaching sculptural constructions to them to alter the body's natural shape. He then further transforms his dancers by flooding them with patterns of light and shadow so that audiences cannot tell what is dancer and what is scenery, what is illusion and what is reality. Through these devices, Nikolais hopes to transcend the limitations of ordinary theater and to extend the possibilities of the human anatomy.

One of the most controversial and influential choreographic experimentalists is Merce Cunningham. His performance style is almost balletically elegant, although unlike ballet dancers Cunningham's dancers seldom try to appear ethereal. Despite their latent classicism, Cunningham productions—many of them collaborations with composer John Cage—have prompted extremes of rage and enthusiasm. Three aspects of Cunningham's approach have been especially provocative: his use of chance and indeterminacy; his treatment of stage space as an open field; and his treatment of the elements that comprise a dance production as independent entities. Most notably, Cunningham uses chance elements in compositions so that his dances will possess some of the unpredictability of life itself. But he uses them with discretion; his dances are not free-for-alls. For instance, he may prepare in advance a multitude of movement possibilities—more than he needs for a work—and then decide by flipping coins which sequences will actually occur in that work. Or he may create works in which a set number of episodes may be performed in any order.

Both Paul Taylor and Merce Cunningham formerly danced with Martha Graham, a fact that makes their differences as well as their similarities instructive. Both favor unusual amalgams of music and movement, but Taylor's works (among them Book of Beasts, *above*) are often unrestrained and ebullient, whereas Cunningham works such as Rainforest (*shown opposite*) are serenely abstract.

Overleaf: *Cunningham insists that chance and indeterminacy govern his compositions. In fact they are governed by the choreographer's disciplined inventiveness, which imposes its own unity on* Summerspace.

It may be asked why, if Cunningham prepares so much, he bothers with chance at all. Advocates of his method will reply that chance can reveal to the choreographer ways of combining movements which his conscious mind might not otherwise have thought of; our conscious minds are, to an extent, prisoners of habit, prisoners of thought patterns that we have been building up all our lives. By utilizing chance in choreography, it is possible to discover attractive combinations of movements that our conscious minds might not otherwise have thought of on their own.

Concern with indeterminacy is only to be expected in an age where live performances are, in a sense, in subtle competition with such mechanical forms as films and television. One characteristic of the mechanical is its fixity: once something has been captured on film, it will stay that way forever, or at least until the film wears out. But every live performance is different, even if only slightly, from every other live performance. Cunningham merely exploits the element of indeterminacy inherent in all theater.

A second important aspect of Cunningham's approach is his treatment of stage space. Unlike classical ballet, which is often structured around a central focus—usually the ballerina, performing front-and-center, framed by the ensemble—Cunningham gives equal importance to each area of the stage. The corners and sides can be as important as the center, and many things can happen simultaneously in different parts of the stage. The spectator's eye, instead of being riveted to one point, is free to wander as it wishes across a field of activity. There is no necessary reason why this should create difficulties for the spectator, since our eyes are regularly used to assimilate situations of greater visual complexity than can be found in most dances—for example, we readily adjust to the sight of pedestrians in the street or crowds at beaches or in bus stations.

Lastly, Cunningham tends to regard the elements of a work—movement, sound, decor—as independent entities which coexist together. The dance does not attempt to duplicate the musical phrase. Nor does the scenery illustrate the choreography. Choreography, music, and scenery simply occupy time and space together. Yet, oddly enough, these elements, though separate, manage to give each Cunningham work its own special climate. *Rainforest*, for instance, contains lush, sensuous movement; David Tudor's electronic score chugs gently along like a motorboat going up a river; Andy Warhol's decor consists of floating silver pillows. There is nothing specifically tropical about this piece, yet it is thoroughly luxuriant in tone.

The best advice one can give to anyone unfamiliar with Cunningham is simply to forget the theories and watch the dances with a keen eye and open mind. Gradually, each dance will reveal its personality. Thus *Summerspace* shimmers like August heat; *Winterbranch* is filled with so many suggestions of oppression that it frequently reminds audiences of the horrors of war; *Landrover* eats up space with enthusiastic abandon; and *Suite for Five* is as cool as spring water. Cunningham dances are like landscapes; the separate elements in them cohere to produce an unmistakable atmosphere, just as certain aggrega-

131

tions of people, traffic, and buildings are, in appearance, unmistakably those of a city's main street or financial district, its parks or its suburbs.

Since the 1960's there has been an extraordinary resurgence of modern dance experimentation. During the early years of the decade, many dancers performed at New York City's Judson Memorial Church, a Baptist church that has long been concerned with liberal social action and support of the arts (even though the grandmother of one of its ministers once announced that "A praying knee and a dancing foot never grew on the same leg"). Most of the important choreographers associated with Judson have established independent careers, while still other choreographers have conducted their experiments totally apart from the Judson milieu.

Recent experimentation has concentrated upon two broad areas: the kinds of movements that may be used in a dance, and the space in which a dance may be performed. It now appears that virtually any movement from the simplest to the most complex may be legitimately employed by choreographers. Twyla Tharp has on occasion covered space with intricate webs of nimble, twisting movements. In contrast, Yvonne Rainer has emphasized an athletic roughhouse kind of movement derived from gymnastics and work activities. Several lesser-known choreographers—in a development parallel to minimal painting and sculpture—have choreographed pieces with people assembling and dispersing in geometrical formations and have deliberately cast them with nondancers so that they will have a realistic appearance.

Going to another extreme, James Waring has been wildly eclectic. He has combined Bach and 1920's pop songs within a single piece, while other works include florid pantomimes, austere abstractions, tributes to Jeanette MacDonald movies, and romantic ballets *en pointe*. He roams from period to period with a genuine affection that makes him want to revivify the past. He demonstrates that any style can be theatrically valid, provided a choreographer treats it with respect. Other choreographers juxtapose many kinds of movement in dances: Rudy Perez uses movement which seems rich in emotional implications but which he measures out with tight, stoic control; Murray Louis is the master of a peppery comic style; while Dan Wagoner often plays perception games with audiences. In Wagoner's *Brambles*, for example, a live dancer performs while another person describes him in relation to totally imaginary scenery.

Just as any kind of movement may be used in a dance, so dances may be given in all kinds of spaces. The spaces in which dances are being presented today include churches, gymnasiums, armories, museums, parks, and city streets. And these areas are being used for their own sake, not as second-best substitutes for conventional theaters. Twyla Tharp once produced an event called *Medley* at twilight in New York City's Central Park. Its most striking episode was its conclusion, in which forty-odd dancers were spread across the grass, some near the audience, others almost as far away as the eye could see. All performed identical steps, but each was told to dance them as slowly as he personally could. Some moved so slowly that it was not always possible to discern if they were moving at all. In the fading light the

Lark Ascending is Ailey's paean to the unchecked, airborne human spirit, loosed from the fetters of oppression, ignorance, and tyranny. Opposite, Sara Yarborough, a company principal, soars through the lead role.

almost imperceptible movement suggested a sculpture garden come magically to life.

Among young choreographers, Meredith Monk has been particularly interested in environmental theater productions staged on lawns, in empty lots, and in the interiors of museums and churches. She utilized New York's Solomon R. Guggenheim Museum for *Juice*, in which dancers moved along the great spiral interior ramp designed by Frank Lloyd Wright. Set in the vast nave of the Cathedral of St. John the Divine, *Education of the Girl Child* showed the course of life from

birth to old age, then reversed the process and unwound life from old age back to birth. In *Needle Brain Lloyd and the Systems Kid*, Monk filled the Connecticut College lawn with a zany assortment of characters that included croquet players, mobsters, pioneers, and a motorcycle gang.

A form of dance that has been attracting ever wider attention is black dance, a choreographic amalgam of elements derived from jazz and tap, from conventional modern dance, and from the history and traditions of Africa, the Caribbean, the American South, and the big-city ghetto. The result is a dance form of tremendous energy, fervor, and rage. Pioneers of black dance include Asadata Dafora Horton, who in the 1930's created dance dramas about tribal life, and Katherine Dunham and Pearl Primus, who achieved prominence in the 1940's. Dunham treated Caribbean and American black themes in a series of revues that were exuberant combinations of scholarly research and

It was Agnes de Mille who discovered Judith Jamison in Philadelphia in 1964 and invited her to join A.B.T., but it is Alvin Ailey who has guided her to her greatest triumphs. The most galvanic of these is Cry, *an idealized but unsentimental tribute to black women that Ailey created for Jamison in 1971.* Cry *is one of the most arduous solos ever choreographed. It is also one of the most overwhelming—and when Jamison danced it (above) for the first time, her audience responded with an ovation that sounded "like an ocean."*

showbiz flair. Primus's repertoire ranged from recreations of African ceremonies to *Strange Fruit*, which concerned lynching in the South. Both Dunham and Primus are university-trained anthropologists as well as choreographers.

Notable compositions on black themes created since the 1950's include Talley Beatty's *Road of the Phoebe Snow*, based upon childhood memories of games, fights, and dances along the railroad tracks; and Donald McKayle's *Rainbow Round My Shoulder*, depicting convicts on the chain gang, and *District Storyville*, a look at New Orleans

in the early days of jazz when musicians earned their living by playing in brothels. One of the most popular American dance companies is that of Alvin Ailey. Like the New York City Ballet and the Joffrey Ballet, it is affiliated with the New York City Center. Its repertoire contains Ailey's own rousing *Revelations*, set to spirituals, and an assortment of works by many choreographers, black and white.

Modern dance remains volatile. No one can ever predict what the next trend will be, but one can assume there will be constant stylistic changes. Increasingly, modern dance and ballet, once bitter rivals, are regarding each other with cordial respect. Many dancers are now versed in both idioms, and several modern dance works have been taken into ballet repertoires. But even as the innovations of one era of modern dance are being assimilated by the dance world as a whole, new choreographers are breaking fresh ground. Modern dance would not be modern if it were not in a state of constant ferment.

9

Contemporary Kaleidoscope

Sir Frederick Ashton has proved to be one of the most versatile of twentieth-century choreographers. In his nearly forty-year association with the company now known as the Royal Ballet, Ashton produced every type of dance—pieces ranging from airy comedy to brooding tragedy. In the photograph opposite, Merle Park and Anthony Dowell perform a pas de deux *from Ashton's 1946 abstract masterpiece,* Symphonic Variations.

TODAY DANCE FLOURISHES in virtually every corner of the world. Most major cities possess companies of some kind, and surprisingly many possess important companies. Dance is an art blessedly free of language barriers, yet each place where it thrives develops its own stylistic accent. England, for example, can point with pride to several remarkable national companies, led by the Royal Ballet. Interestingly enough, despite its name the Royal Ballet's origins were in fact exceedingly humble. The conditions of British dance early in our century closely resembled those that prevailed in the United States at the time, which is to say that both countries welcomed foreign dancers but few attempts were made to found native companies. Many people, including balletomanes, felt that dancing was best left to the Russians or the French. Fortunately, some strong-minded women disagreed.

One such woman was born in Ireland in 1898. Her real name—Edris Stannus—is resoundingly Irish, but she is better known by her equally resounding stage name, Ninette de Valois. After dancing with the Diaghilev ballet for several seasons, she left the company in 1925 and started teaching in England, where she also became involved with several struggling repertory theaters. These theaters were invariably high-minded; just as invariably, they were poverty-stricken, unfashionable, and situated in remote neighborhoods. No wonder de Valois's mother once asked her despairingly why she always had to work on "the wrong side of the river."

Among the theaters that hired de Valois was London's Old Vic, located on the shabby side of the Thames. Under the guidance of Lilian Baylis, this remarkable center offered drama and opera at the lowest possible prices. De Valois soon persuaded Baylis to sponsor ballet as well. And when the latter opened a second theater, the long-derelict Sadler's Wells, in 1931, de Valois became director of the Vic-Wells Ballet—which, as its name suggests, performed alternately at the two theaters. Later, the Old Vic was used exclusively for drama and the ballet company became the Sadler's Wells Ballet, a name it retained when it moved to the Royal Opera House after World War II. By the 1950's de Valois's group was numbered among the great companies of the world, and in 1956 it received a royal charter and a new name, the Royal Ballet. Unlike other royal companies of Europe, Britain's Royal Ballet was not founded as a toy for aristocrats. Instead, it was the outgrowth of a genuine community theater movement.

There were dancegoers—particularly some fans of Colonel de Basil's Ballet Russe—who scoffed at the young Vic-Wells, but the company also had many admirers. In 1933, for instance, the Camargo Society, an organization dedicated to the sponsorship of new British ballet productions, turned over all its funds to the Vic-Wells. The main reason for the company's success was the fortitude and vision of its director, however. Although de Valois's choreographic output diminished as her administrative duties increased, three of her ballets survive. *Checkmate* depicts an allegorical chess game between love and death. Two other extant works derive from British art: *Job*, which is based upon Blake's illustrations of the biblical story, and *The Rake's Progress*, modeled upon Hogarth and showing a fashionable young man's descent into debauchery. When de Valois retired as director in 1964, she was succeeded by Frederick Ashton, who in turn was succeeded in 1970 by Kenneth MacMillan, a choreographer who was trained at the Sadler's Wells Ballet School.

Never a glamorous figure, de Valois has commonly impressed observers as being firm, even prim, in manner, and it has been suggested that if she had not been a ballet director she could well have been a governess—or a member of Parliament. Quite different is another great lady of British ballet, the tempestuous Marie Rambert, whose real name is Cyvia Rambam and who was born in Warsaw in 1888. The daughter of well-read parents, she shares the family blessing of literacy and the family curse of insomnia. Her parents read *War and Peace* aloud when they could not sleep, and Rambert often occupies her own sleepless nights by reciting poetry to herself in several languages. She was a fidgety child, and as she grew up her restlessness expressed itself in radical politics. Her parents, afraid that her revolutionary sentiments might get her into trouble, sent her to Paris to study.

There, in a roundabout fashion, Rambert was to become involved with ballet. Her first idol was Isadora Duncan—a significant influence, for Rambert has always been interested in choreographic innovation. Her initial training, however, was in eurhythmics, the method of rhythmic analysis devised by Dalcroze. And it was because of her knowledge of eurhythmics that Diaghilev hired her to help Nijinsky understand Stravinsky's puzzling score for *Le Sacre du Printemps*. Working with the Diaghilev company, she acquired a respect for ballet. (She also apparently fell in love with Nijinsky, though she did not dare admit it.) Later, Rambert settled in London and opened a ballet school.

Among Rambert's many talents, two have attracted widespread attention. One is an ability to turn cartwheels. Until her seventieth birthday, Rambert turned cartwheels everywhere, including around the Salzburg Mozart memorial and in Trafalgar Square. As an elderly woman, she regrets the loss of this ability and assures skeptics that cartwheels do wonders to clear the brain. Rambert's other gift—her ability to guide young choreographers—has of course had a more significant influence on dance history. It was Rambert who persuaded Frederick Ashton to choreograph his first ballet in 1926, and it has been Rambert who has developed many new choreographers since the 1930's.

In comparison with the venerable classical ballet companies of Russia, Italy, and France, Great Britain's Royal Ballet is a veritable upstart. Yet through the patience and persistence of its founder, Ninette de Valois (above), and principal choreographer, Frederick Ashton, the Royal Ballet has created a distinctive national style that is recognized throughout the world. Like Balanchine, Ashton has been profoundly influenced by the classicism of Petipa. The British preserve the Petipa legacy in such productions as the revival of La Bayadère *at right, staged by Rudolf Nureyev.*

Early in 1931, Rambert's husband, playwright Ashley Dukes, converted an old parish hall into a theater, which they named the Mercury. There Rambert established the Ballet Club the same year that the Vic-Wells Ballet made its debut. The Ballet Club was no Vic-Wells, however, for the Mercury's stage was scarcely larger than a postage stamp. Moreover, Rambert not only lacked de Valois's organizational powers, she also had a fearful temper. Yet somehow she managed to work magic. She was forever encouraging some young talent, and although

her protégés eventually left to join companies that danced on larger stages, newcomers would always appear. Renamed Ballet Rambert, the company outgrew the Mercury. Now one of the institutions of British ballet, it has never been content to rest on its laurels, and, since 1965, Rambert and her latest choreographic discovery, Norman Morrice, have reorganized the group to stress modern dance.

Surely the greatest talents nurtured by Rambert have been Antony Tudor, who choreographed for the Ballet Club before emigrating to America in 1939, and Frederick Ashton, whose ballets reveal much about the English temperament. Although the latter spent his childhood in South America, his works possess a sweetness of temper and a sense of graciousness and decorum that strike critics as typical and admirable English virtues. In 1935 Ashton joined the Vic-Wells, and his choreography matured along with the company. But it was Rambert who produced his first efforts. An unusually varied choreographer, Ashton has provided serene abstractions (*Symphonic Variations*), pure fantasies (*Cinderella, Ondine,* and *The Dream,* based upon *A Midsummer Night's Dream*), and especially adept comic ballets. Among these last are *A Wedding Bouquet,* which depicts misadventures at a provincial wedding and is accompanied by the recitation of a nonsensical Gertrude Stein text, and a sparkling new version of the eighteenth-century ballet *La Fille Mal Gardée.* One of Ashton's most unusual achievements is *Enigma Variations,* which, combining tenderness with realistic detail, offers portraits of the composer Edward Elgar and his friends. It evokes the Edwardian period so convincingly that one sighs that time has separated us eternally from that placid, secure age.

The ballerina for whom Ashton created many lyrical roles—and the dancer who remains one of the best exemplars of his style—is Margot Fonteyn. She joined the Vic-Wells during the 1934–35 season, and during the next quarter-century she was partnered by such British-trained dancers as Robert Helpmann, Michael Somes, and David Blair. Since the 1960's, however, she has been associated with Russian-born Rudolf Nureyev, and the combination of her quiet radiance and his magnetic stage presence has made theirs one of the outstanding partnerships in contemporary ballet. Other major exemplars of Ashton's lyric style include Antoinette Sibley and Anthony Dowell.

Serious British dance, like serious American dance, is a relatively recent phenomenon. In Russia, on the other hand, dance is heir to a long and proud tradition, one that has survived not only changing taste but drastic changes of government. The Russian Revolution of 1917, for instance, inspired wild artistic experimentation. It also encouraged cultural iconoclasm, and this in turn led some zealots, who regarded ballet as a relic of tsarist tyranny, to seek to destroy it utterly. Others, ultimately triumphant, sought to modify its techniques to meet the demands of Soviet society. Considering industrialism as a means for saving humanity from want, several choreographers became obsessed by machines and tried to make human movement imitate the action of pistons and conveyor belts. One choreographer stated, "The Muses have become production workers and dispersed into trade unions." Overseeing the development of ballet was Anatoly Lunacharsky, first

During the 1960's Rudolf Nureyev's partnership with British ballerina Margot Fonteyn was one of the stellar attractions of the dance world, and many ballets were created especially for the two, among them Ashton's Marguerite and Armand, *seen at right. For Fonteyn the alliance with Nureyev represented the capstone of a career that spanned more than four decades and was highlighted by associations with such other outstanding dancers as Robert Helpmann, Michael Somes, and David Blair (below).*

Overleaf: *The American Ballet Theatre in two contrasting moods: at left, the casual atmosphere of a pre-performance warm-up; at right, the courtly ritual of the curtain call.*

Soviet Commissar of Education, who managed to encourage experimentation without ever acceding to the extremists who were demanding ballet's abolition.

Two Russian choreographers earned reputations as innovators during this period. The first, Fyodor Lopukhov, combined ballet with acrobatics. His *Dance Symphony* (1923) was an essentially abstract composition that purported to express the splendor of the universe. His cast included the young George Balanchine, whose own taste may have been influenced by Lopukhov. Balanchine also admired Kasian Goleizovsky, who, like Lopukhov, utilized acrobatics and whose choreography, in its day, was considered highly erotic. Neither Lopukhov nor Goleizovsky ever really dominated Russian ballet, however. Indications of the course Soviet ballet did take may be found in *The Red Poppy*, choreographed by Vassily Tikhomirov and Lev Laschilin in 1927, and *Flames of Paris*, choreographed by Vassily Vainonen in 1932. The latter concerns the French Revolution, while the former shows Chinese workers being aided by Russian sailors during a popular uprising. *The Red Poppy* has a rousing score by Glière and one of its tunes, the "Russian Sailors' Dance," still turns up on concert programs. Since the 1930's, the norm of Soviet ballet has been the evening-length narrative, often derived from history and literature and featuring vigorous action and heroic or optimistic themes. Leading examples of Soviet narrative ballet include Rostislav Zakharov's *The Fountain of Bakhshisarai* (1934), taken from Pushkin, and Leonide Lavrovsky's *Romeo and Juliet* (1940), with its distinguished score by Prokofiev. More recently, Yuri Grigorovich has been praised for choreographing such ballets as *The Stone Flower*, *Spartacus*, and a new version of *The Nutcracker*.

Soviet choreography gets a mixed reception outside Russia. Praised for its epic sweep, it is also criticized for a tendency toward overstatement. But on one matter there is almost universal assent: everyone agrees that Soviet dancers can be extraordinary. Soviet style stresses elevation, fluid arms, a strong back, and amplitude of movement. Two

Although current Soviet choreography has not met with widespread critical approval outside Russia, few critics would dispute the fact that the Soviet ballet schools continue to produce outstanding dancers. On the opposite page are four of the Bolshoi Ballet's leading performers: Alexander Lapauri in The Fountain of Bakhchisarai *(top); Nina Sorokina in* The Flames of Paris *(center); and Maya Plisetskaya and Nicolai Fadeyechev in* Firebird *(bottom). Italian ballerina Carla Fracci, seen above with Mario Pistoni in* Daphnis and Chloe, *is recognized as one of the leading interpreters of the Romantic repertory.*

ballerinas, both admired in the West, typify the style's virtues: the now-retired Galina Ulanova, whose body could eloquently register the slightest nuances of characterization, and Maya Plisetskaya, celebrated for her zest and dazzle.

A standard teaching method now prevails throughout the U.S.S.R., based upon the pedagogical theories of Agrippina Vaganova, one of the important teachers of our century. Yet despite the official syllabus, local differences nonetheless exist, for just as Moscow and St. Petersburg were balletic rivals in the nineteenth century, so the two cities remain today, and for some of the same basic reasons. Moscow's Bolshoi Ballet prides itself upon its theatrical vividness, while Leningrad's Kirov claims to be unrivaled for purity of line.

The Soviet Union has also encouraged what might be termed folkloric ballet companies, which adapt and edit the folk dances of a region until they attain a theatrically effective shape. The resultant dances inevitably lose some authenticity, but they gain concomitantly in entertainment value. One of the leading folkloric troupes is the State Folk Dance Ensemble, founded in 1937 by Igor Moiseyev, which performs dances from all parts of the U.S.S.R. as well as from some of the many nations it has visited. (The Soviet bloc is not alone in recognizing the value of exporting folklore. Other countries have founded their own folkloric ensembles—for example, Mexico's Ballet Folklórico and the Bayanihan Dance Company of the Philippines.) Purists may argue that such presentations offer only a rosy view of a nation's traditions, yet if that makes them propagandistic, their propaganda is far more fun than political speeches or economic treatises.

When Russia wishes to impress other countries, it often sends its leading dancers there. After the Chinese Revolution, for example, Russian ballet teachers went to China, where they produced such Western classics as *Swan Lake* and *Giselle*. The Sino-Soviet rift forced these classics out of the repertoire, but ballets on topical and historical themes continued to be created in China to inculcate audiences with patriotic feelings. Because China has long been cut off from Western Europe and America, little is known about these works, although two were apparently great successes: *The White-Haired Girl*, about a girl's escape from the cruel landlord who tries to abduct her, and *Red Detachment of Women*, in which a house slave joins a guerrilla band.

Cultural exchanges between East and West have frequently included visits by dance companies. By and large, the world's dancers and dance audiences enjoy a peaceful coexistence that politicians might envy, yet cultural exchange has not been entirely free of tension. It was threatened by the Vietnam War in the late 1960's, and in early 1974 a proposed American tour of the Kirov Ballet was canceled largely because of the uproar occasioned by the refusal of Soviet authorities to let Valery Panov, one of the Kirov's leading dancers, emigrate to Israel with his wife. (Bowing to international pressure, the Russian government relented in June of that year and the Panovs were permitted to depart for the West.) Despite such incidents, dancers continue to be among the true internationalists of the world, their art refusing to recognize any boundaries.

Russia is a country that has successfully adapted its dance traditions for a new era. Other nations have tried to make similar adaptations—with varying results. Italy, though it continues to train fine individual dancers, has declined in importance. The Royal Danish Ballet preserves its Bournonville legacy and constantly adds items to the repertoire, but Denmark has never found another choreographer equal to August Bournonville.

As for France—well, as often happens in artistic matters, France constitutes a special case. At the end of the nineteenth century the Paris Opéra Ballet sank into a lethargy from which it was roused in 1929 by the arrival of choreographer Serge Lifar. Lifar, a former member of Diaghilev's company, dominated Parisian dance for more than three decades. A strikingly proportioned dancer, a *bon vivant* fond of mingling with high society, and an indefatigable choreographer, he had the knack of being the center of attention, no matter what the circumstances were. As a theorist, Lifar believed that in ballet productions the choreographer was apt to become subordinate to the composer and the designer. Therefore, like the early modern dancers, Lifar proclaimed

Although schooled in the classical tradition of the Paris Opéra Ballet, Roland Petit broke away from that style to create vividly sensual ballets for Les Ballets des Champs-Elysées and the Ballets de Paris de Roland Petit. Following a second, equally successful career in motion pictures and musical revues, Petit returned to the Paris Opéra, where he choreographed such intriguing works as Turangalila, *above.*

dance an autonomous art and, on occasion, as with his *Icare* of 1935, he created his entire ballet in advance and only then noted down the choreographic rhythms and sent them to be orchestrated by an obliging composer. Yet just as certain French vintages do not travel well, so Lifar's choreography is not always to everyone's taste. The qualities which Parisian balletgoers admire as "stylish" are sometimes considered mannered elsewhere.

Several attempts have been made to develop French ballet beyond the Opéra's precincts. Diaghilev's secretary, Boris Kochno, founded Les Ballets des Champs-Elysées in 1945 with the support of Jean Cocteau and designer Christian Bérard. Until it was disbanded in 1951, the company delighted audiences with a freshness and chic which suggested that smart stylishness had returned to postwar Europe. Kochno encouraged two choreographers, Janine Charrat and Roland Petit, and Petit's *Le Jeune Homme et la Mort*, choreographed under Cocteau's supervision, was one of the company's triumphs. In this curious ballet, a young man, scorned by his sweetheart, commits suicide. The personification of Death arrives to claim him. Removing her mask, Death reveals herself to be the young woman of the previous scene. Together, the two walk away across the rooftops of Paris. Not the least surprising thing about the piece was its music. The ballet was rehearsed to jazz and it was only on the day of the premiere that the cast learned that the actual score was to be a Bach passacaglia—the nobility of Bach's music serving as ironic counterpoint to the sordid action.

In 1948 Petit founded his own Ballets de Paris, for which he created works audiences found titillating, even risqué. The most talked-about was a version of *Carmen* starring his wife Renée ("Zizi") Jeanmaire. Petit has since staged dances for films and musical revues, as well as for French and foreign ballet troupes.

France has given birth to a multitude of companies, each with its own distinctive personality. The most lavish was Le Grand Ballet du Marquis de Cuevas. In the century of the welfare state, this constituted almost an anachronism, for it was a large company run at the whim of a Chilean-born nobleman of Spanish extraction whose wife happened to be John D. Rockefeller's granddaughter. A fantastic, almost improbable personage, the marquis lived in theatrical style, was impeccably polite, dispensed kisses so liberally that local wits nicknamed him the "kissing marquis," and even participated in some well-staged, well-publicized, and ultimately harmless duels. To no one's surprise, the marquis's company did not long survive his death in 1961. More recent French ballet activities include attempts to promote dance in regional centers. The Marseille Opéra Ballet has been especially active, while Ballet Théâtre Contemporain of Angers stresses collaboration with contemporary composers and artists.

Today's most controversial French choreographer resides in Belgium. Maurice Béjart and his Brussels-based Ballet of the Twentieth Century rank among the real phenomena of contemporary ballet. Béjart is known for his beautiful dancers and for productions that tackle complex social and philosophical issues. In his version of *Firebird*, for instance, the title character is not a ballerina but the male leader of guerrilla partisans; *Romeo and Juliet* uses Shakespeare's story to preach a "make love, not war" message; while the Béjart interpretation of *Le Sacre du Printemps* is high in both energy level and erotic content. Frequently, Béjart composes spectacles for vast arenas or amphitheaters, his treatment of Beethoven's Ninth Symphony being a plea for brotherhood, his *Nijinsky* offering a phantasmagoric biography of the Russian dancer. Audience reaction to such works fluctuates wildly: some dancegoers admire the physicality of Béjart's dancers, the topicality of his themes, and his pictorially effective groupings; others find Béjart's choreography repetitive and lacking in subtlety. Whatever a viewer's reaction may be, it tends to be strong. Few people are neutral about Béjart.

Although his works in no way resembled those of Béjart, John Cranko also prompted controversy. The South African choreographer's first successes were with Sadler's Wells Ballet, but he achieved international prominence when he assumed the direction of the Stuttgart Ballet in 1960, putting Stuttgart back on the ballet map for the first

The massive spectacles presented by Maurice Béjart's Ballet of the Twentieth Century recall the style of early dance entertainments with their rich admixture of costume, color, and movement. Béjart places a special emphasis on the visual component of his work, as is evidenced by the striking pose taken by dancers of the La Scala Company during a performance of Béjart's Firebird (below). Richly costumed revivals of classics such as The Sleeping Beauty (left) were a trademark of Marquis de Cuevas's now defunct Grand Ballet.

time since Noverre had been ballet master there in the eighteenth century. Cranko's most frequently discussed productions were evening-long adaptations from familiar literary sources—*Romeo and Juliet, Eugene Onegin, The Taming of the Shrew, Carmen.* Their fans admired them for clarity of characterization and swiftness of action, while their critics accused them of being dramatically obvious and choreographically thin. Yet both admirers and detractors lauded Cranko as an astute director, and his untimely death in 1973 on his way home from an American tour came as a shock to the entire ballet world.

Though the Stuttgart is the best-known troupe, all the leading German cities have ballet companies attached to their opera houses or municipal theaters. This German ballet boom has largely occurred since World War II, for before the war Germany favored modern dance. But modern dance withered during the Nazi years and after the war Germans turned to ballet as one way in which they could rejoin the world cultural community. Performance standards differ from city to city, but several groups are highly competent, and simply because there

are so many companies—all clamoring for new ballets—Germany offers a myriad of employment opportunities for foreign choreographers. For instance, the young American choreographer John Neumeier has done almost all of his work in Germany.

Until recently, European dancers, teachers, and choreographers would go to America to promote ballet there. Now America sends dance abroad. American ballet has impressed the Continent, while American modern dance, for which most foreign nations have no equivalent, has been influential in England, Germany, Holland, and Israel. One American modern dance choreographer, Glen Tetley, has been so successful overseas that he is almost better known in Europe than he is in his native land. In 1974 he was appointed director of the Stuttgart Ballet, succeeding John Cranko.

Scanning the dance map of the world, one finds companies in Norway and Sweden, and in South Africa and Japan. Prague and Budapest love ballet, as do Vienna, Zurich, Geneva, Amsterdam, and The Hague. Ballet exists throughout Latin America, and the British Commonwealth can lay claim to the Australian Ballet, the National Ballet of Canada, Les Grands Ballets Canadiens of Montreal, and, finally, the Royal Winnipeg Ballet.

Underlying the growth in popularity of ballet today is its ability to embrace both the old and new in dance expression. Classics such as The Nutcracker *(above) remain the backbone of ballet repertory, but experimental choreography also flourishes. American choreographer Glen Tetley, the director of the Stuttgart Ballet, is among the experimenters who have deftly mixed modern dance techniques with traditional ballet steps in such works as* Laborintus *(opposite).*

Overleaf: *Massed dancers and chorus present Maurice Béjart's interpretation of Beethoven's Ninth Symphony.*

It is somehow invigorating to be where there is dancing, even as a spectator. Dancers invariably seem more nimble than other people, just as dance can be more vivacious than most other arts. Dance unites grace and prowess, elegance and strength, body and spirit. Styles change, steps are modified, traditions are conserved or defied, yet the appeal of dance remains that of watching bodies move in time and space.

Scarcely four centuries have elapsed since Catherine de Médicis and her courtiers sat in galleried halls to watch the spectacles which marked the beginning of the performing tradition that includes ballet and modern dance. In those centuries dance has moved from the palace to the theater and, occasionally, out of the theater and into streets and stadiums. Dancers have worn heavy robes, filmy tutus, toe shoes, tights, and sometimes nothing at all. They have impersonated the gods and conjured up spirits, they have leaped through the air and crawled on the ground, they have explored the darkest corners of the psyche and have at times been content to be nothing more than themselves—beautiful beings in elegant motion.

A lot has happened in four centuries. And yet when compared with drama or poetry—which can trace their histories back for thousands of years—ballet and modern dance are very young arts indeed. They have accomplished much in such a short time, and who knows what they may accomplish in the future. Perhaps their greatest days still lie ahead. Perhaps the history of dance has only begun.

DANCERS AND THE DANCE

Isadora Duncan's fame did not rest entirely upon her dancing. In all matters of style and social convention, she lived outside the mainstream, whether judged by the standards of her native land, the United States, or her adopted home, France. Janet Flanner, an American living in Paris at the time of Isadora's death, was one of many writers touched by the magnificence of Isadora's personality, which Flanner poignantly recaptured in a eulogy that appeared in The New Yorker.

In the summer of 1926, like a ghost from the grave, Isadora Duncan began dancing again in Nice. Two decades before, her art, animated by her extraordinary public personality, came as close to founding an aesthetic renaissance as American morality would allow, and the provinces especially had a narrow escape. But in the postwar European years her body, whose Attic splendor once brought Greece to Kansas and Kalamazoo, was approaching its half-century mark. Her spirit was still green as a bay tree, but her flesh was worn, perhaps by the weight of laurels. She was the last of the trilogy of great female personalities our century cherished. Two of them, Duse and Bernhardt, had already gone to their elaborate national tombs. Only Isadora Duncan, the youngest, the American, remained wandering the foreign earth. . . .

As an artist, Isadora made her appearance in our plain and tasteless republic before the era of the half-nude revue, before the discovery of what is now called our Native Literary School, even before the era of the celluloid sophistication of the cinema, which by its ubiquity does so much to unite the cosmopolitanisms of Terre Haute and New York. What America now has, and gorges on in the way of sophistication, it then hungered for. Repressed by generations of Puritanism, it longed for bright, visible, and blatant beauty presented in a public form the simple citizenry could understand. Isadora appeared as a half-clothed Greek. . . .

A Paris *couturier* once said woman's modern freedom in dress is largely due to Isadora. She was the first artist to appear uncinctured, barefooted, and free. She arrived like a glorious bounding Minerva in the midst of a cautious corseted decade. The clergy, hearing of (though supposedly without ever seeing) her bare calf, denounced it as violently as if it had been golden. Despite its longings, for a moment America hesitated, Puritanism rather than poetry coupling lewd with nude in rhyme. But Isadora, originally from California and by then from Berlin, Paris, and other points, arrived bearing her gifts as a Greek. She came like a figure from the Elgin marbles. The world over, and in America particularly, Greek sculpture was recognized to be almost notorious for its purity. The overpowering sentiment for Hellenic culture, even in the unschooled United States, silenced the outcries. Isadora had come as antique art and with such backing she became a cult.

Those were Isadora's great years. Not only in New York and Chicago but in the smaller, harder towns, when she moved across the stage,

The sketch above, like those on pages 157–79, is by Edgar Degas, a lifelong devotee of classical dance.

head reared, eyes mad, scarlet kirtle flying to the music of the "Marseillaise," she lifted from their seats people who had never left theater seats before except to get up and go home. . . .

In order to promulgate her pedagogic theories of beauty and education for the young, she legally adopted and supported some thirty or forty children during her life. . . . During her famous season at the New York Century Theatre where she gave a classic Greek cycle, *Oedipus Rex*, *Antigone*, and the like, she bought up every Easter lily in Manhattan to decorate the theater the night she opened in Berlioz's *L'Enfance du Christ*, which was her Easter program. The lilies, whose perfume suffocated the spectators, cost two thousand dollars. Isadora had, at the moment, three thousand dollars to her name. And at midnight, long after all good lily-selling florists were in bed, she gave a champagne supper. It cost the other thousand. . . .

After the lilies faded, Isadora and her school sat amid their luggage on the pier where the ship was about to sail for France. They had neither tickets nor money. But they had a classic faith in fate and a determination to go back to Europe, where art was understood. Just before the boat sailed, there appeared a schoolteacher. Isadora had never seen her before. The teacher gave Isadora the savings of years and Isadora sailed away. Herself grand, she could inspire grandeur in others, a tragic and tiring gift. There were always schoolteachers and lilies in Isadora's life. . . .

. . . an integral part of Isadora's nature died young when her two adored little children, Deirdre and Patrick, were tragically drowned in 1913 at Neuilly; the automobile in which they were waiting alone slipped its brakes and plunged into the Seine. The children had been the offspring of free unions, in which Isadora spiritedly believed. She believed, too, in polyandry and that each child thus benefited eugenically by having a different and carefully chosen father. She also attributed the loss of her third child, born the day war was declared, to what she called the curse of the machine. At the wild report that the Germans were advancing by motor on Paris, the old Bois de Boulogne gates were closed, her doctor and his automobile, amidst thousands of cars, were caught behind the grill, and by the time he arrived at her bedside it was too late. The child had been born dead. "Machines have been my enemy," she once said. "They killed my three children. Machines are the opposite of, since they are the invention of, man. Perhaps a machine will one day kill me."

In a moment of melancholy her friend Duse prophesied that Isadora would die like Jocasta. Both prophecies were fulfilled. On August 13, 1927, while driving on the Promenade des Anglais at Nice, Isadora Duncan met her death. She was strangled by her colored shawl, which became tangled in the wheel of the automobile. . . .

All her life Isadora had been a practical idealist. She had put into practice certain ideals of art, maternity, and political liberty which people prefer to read as theories on paper. Her ideals of human liberty were not unsimilar to those of Plato, to those of Shelley, to those of Lord Byron, which led him to die dramatically in Greece. All they gained for Isadora were the loss of her passport and the presence of the constabulary on the stage of the Indianapolis Opera House, where the chief of police watched for sedition in the movement of Isadora's knees. . . .

Great artists are tragic. Genius is too large, and it may have been grandeur that proved Isadora's undoing—the grandeur of temporary luxury, the grandeur of permanent ideals.

She was too expansive for personal salvation. She had thousands of friends. What she needed was an organized government. She had had checkbooks. Her scope called for a national treasury. It was not for nothing that she was hailed by her first name only, as queens have been, were they great Catherines or Marie Antoinettes.

As she stepped into the machine that was to be her final enemy, Isadora's last spoken words were, by chance, *"Je vais à la gloire!"*

JANET FLANNER
The New Yorker, 1927

Isadora Duncan stands among the first rank of pioneering talents in modern dance. Working separately, but in similar directions, Loie Fuller, Ruth St. Denis, Ted Shawn, Mary Wigman, and Duncan broke away from the confines of ballet's methodology to find new outlets for self-expression in dance. Duncan, in particular, practiced a highly idiosyncratic art and consequently none of her dances survives in the repertory of modern dance companies today. What has endured, however, is Duncan's approach to movement, the development of which she recorded in her autobiography, published posthumously in 1927.

I spent long days and nights in the studio seeking that dance which might be the divine expression of the human spirit through the medium of the body's movement. For hours I would stand quite still, my two hands folded between my breasts, covering the solar plexus. My mother often became alarmed to see me remain for such long intervals quite motionless as if in a trance—but I was seeking and finally discovered the central spring of all movement, the crater of motor power, the unity from which all diversions of movements are born, the mirror of vision for the creation of the dance—it was from this discovery that was born the theory on which I founded my school. The ballet school taught the pupils that this spring was found in the centre of the back at the base of the spine. From this axis, says the ballet master, arms, legs and trunk must move freely, giving the result of an articulated puppet. This method produces an artificial mechanical movement not worthy of the soul. I on the contrary sought the source of the spiritual expression to flow into the channels of the body filling it with vibrating light —the centrifugal force reflecting the spirit's vision. After many months, when I had learned to concentrate all my force to this one Centre I found that thereafter when I listened to music the rays and vibrations of the music streamed to this one fount of light within me—there they reflected themselves in Spiritual Vision not the brain's mirror, but the soul's, and from this vision I could express them in Dance....

It would seem as if it were a very difficult thing to explain in words, but when I stood before my class of even the smallest and poorest children and said: "Listen to the music with your soul. Now, while listening, do you not feel an inner self awakening deep within you—that it is by its strength that your head is lifted, that your arms are raised, that you are walking slowly toward the light?" they understood. This awakening is the first step in the dance, as I conceive it.

Isadora Duncan
My Life, 1927

Because Giselle *represents the ultimate refinement of Romantic taste and sensibility, it survives in the repertory of contemporary ballet companies and is among the most demanding roles a ballerina can essay. During her long and successful career, Alicia Markova danced* Giselle *frequently and with great distinction. However, few of those later performances could have matched the challenge and excitement that attended the first* Giselle *ever danced by a British ballerina.*

As a romantic setting, North Kensington leaves much to be desired. Even in the nineteen-thirties, the tall converted houses and drab porticos had, at best, an air of faded elegance, as though the ghost of a horse and carriage might be waiting here and there. When Carlotta Grisi danced in London, the district had been an 'exclusive' one, second only to the West End. But time makes strange patterns, and I cannot claim that the furnished rooms where I lived with my mother and sisters after my father's death, were an ideal bower for a Giselle in waiting! For one thing, they did not pretend to be soundproof, and the very night before I danced the great rôle, my reverently-planned hours of sleep were cut to shreds by a cheerful New Year's Eve party in the upstairs flat. I had been invited to it, and for the rest I got, I might just as well have gone....

But as late autumn leaves rustled about the pavements and I took the bus each day to Sadler's Wells Theatre in Islington, I doubt if any surroundings could have quenched my spirits. For even amid fog and drizzle, I had the thrill of knowing that I stood on the threshold of an entirely new career. Eight years ago, the Diaghilev Ballet had opened the door to a fabulous world for me. That closed irrevocably with Diaghilev's death, but now another door had opened and stood wide. Beyond was a new life, all unexplored, with Giselle as its immediate prize.

The formal contract offered to me by the Vic-Wells Company from September 1933 to May 1934, carried a salary of only ten pounds a week, to include my services as *prima ballerina* and my help as choreographer when necessary. Out of this I had to pay many expenses, such as costumes, tights and ballet shoes, and the result was bound to be a rather unglamorous counting of pennies which bore no resemblance to the lot of *prima ballerinas* in magazine fiction! Yet I knew that to engage a resident ballerina at all, was a huge step forward for a young company which functioned on a shoestring! During the previous year, I had earned money where I could, taking commercial dancing engagements at the Regal Cinema, Marble Arch, the Alhambra Theatre, and so on. This made it just possible for me to appear for a token payment each performance with the British ballet groups whose artistic enterprise was so near my heart. These were the Ballet Rambert, Vic-Wells, and, so long as it existed, the Camargo Society. Now that the Vic-Wells had reached Company status, I felt tremendous pride in this appointment as its first *prima ballerina*, and determined to show that a British dancer could succeed in the great classical rôles. Now, however, I had to give up the more lucrative outside work, for Vic-Wells was beginning a tremendous programme. *Giselle*, in fact, turned out to be the first of three major revivals, all mounted for me in 1934, the others being *Nutcracker* and *Swan Lake*. . . .

. . . through the good offices of Lydia Lopokova, Ninette de Valois, Director of the Vic-Wells Ballet engaged Nicolai Sergueeff to stage *Giselle* for the Company and teach me the structure of the role. Sergueeff, who had been living in Paris in poor circumstances as a White Russian refugee, was probably glad of the commission. But the gain certainly was ours too, for he had spent his life in the world of traditional ballet, and his written notations and music scores of many of the great classics were priceless, for they could not be obtained elsewhere. He had been Régisseur of the Maryinsky Theatre in St Petersburg, and afterwards worked with Diaghilev on the classical revivals. Now the written notation of *Giselle* was in his hand when we met, at ten o'clock sharp, in the Board Room of Sadler's Wells Theatre these cold mornings. Here I learned the basic steps, the choreography of *Giselle*.

Despite his romantic links with the great ballets, Sergueeff's personality did not suggest theatrical flair or a vivid imagination. He never coloured his teaching to describe what he felt about *Giselle* as a character, but remained dry and practical, sticking to the notation book. Should I fail to grasp a point, he would bring this and open it before me, for, as he spoke no English and only a little French, discussion was limited. He was, apparently, conventional in outlook and I think it was his strong reaction to the idea of Pavlova-type draperies for the second act of *Giselle*, which caused us to revert to the time-honoured Romantic tutu! But in this his instinct may have been right. Anyway, his notation of *Giselle* was the essential scaffolding on which to build the rôle and make our production possible. And looking back, I see a kind of wisdom in his deliberate policy of not interpreting the rôle for me, because through this I was forced to use my insight and begin to form my own idea of Giselle's character.

Much work was involved in learning the choreography of this Maryinsky production. For example, there would sometimes be two different versions of one particular ménage, or group of steps. Both were equally valid, and both had been popularized by famous ballerinas. Which should I use? Giselle's variation in the first act was a case in point. Tamara Karsavina had danced one version, Olga Spessivtzeva another. Sergueeff gave me my choice here, and I adopted Spessivtzeva's....

Sergueeff and I worked for several hours each morning. Then, after a quick sandwich lunch, we joined the Company for rehearsals in the large first-floor room, now the coffee room. Here I would work through until six. Afterwards, Ninette de Valois and I would often go into the West End to have supper, discuss the progress of the ballet, and sometimes see a film for relaxation. During these weeks, we had comparatively few public performances at the theatre, and so it was possible to devote full attention to the great project of *Giselle*.

Little by little, the production was taking shape. There was no question of anything lavish, for once again, finances simply were not available. I discussed my costume for Act One with Barbara Allen, a young designer then on the staff of Vic-Wells. We could not, it was felt, go far wrong here, for the traditional model was clearly shown in prints and photographs. I had a white organdie skirt of Romantic length, edged with fairly bright blue; a small blue apron and blue bodice, both trimmed with red velvet. The hair style for Act One was the single thing I copied from Spessivtzeva. My hair was then long, and I clasped it back, unbraided, with an old-fashioned slide. A broad blue ribbon, taken round the head as a turban, kept the top part neat. In later productions, of course, I have dressed my hair with clustered or wreathed flowers but in those early days, I felt the headband was practical. For Act Two, I made myself a wreath of tiny ice-blue flowers and touched their petal-tips with paint—with simple 'wet-white', I believe—to give a translucent effect. This habit of improvising head-dresses has stayed with me always, and it may be a legacy from the Diaghilev Ballet, where dancers were always expected to create such things for themselves if the design were simple; for example, one would simply be given a piece of ribbon and a rope of stage pearls and told to make an oriental turban!

In my partner, my first Albrecht, Anton Dolin, I felt that I was fortunate; for it was he who had danced Albrecht to Spessivtzeva's *Giselle* at the Savoy Theatre. She had taught him a great deal about the ballet, and he in turn was able to guide me through the performance....

Partnering in ballet is a subtle art, and I think it is safe to say that an audience seldom realises half the factors involved. All depends upon teamwork, indeed, on super teamwork. There are moments when the ballerina must 'carry the load' and others when her partner should relieve her. The art consists in not letting the audience see which is working hardest at a particular time! A partnership should be so close in mutual understanding that all technical points, even perfect timing, are taken for granted and put out of mind. The *danseur noble* must know what his ballerina is trying to achieve, and so help her to heighten the effect. All this leads to a shared pleasure in accomplishment, which is unique. . . .

. . . Inevitably, the great day came. This performance was to be given at the Old Vic in the Waterloo Road, already famous for its Shakespearian productions. By the previous evening, every normal detail of our *Giselle* seemed to be under control. Was I? I have already mentioned the New Year's Eve party which tore my rest to tatters! Instead of the soft lights and sweet music which one might feel to be a fitting overture for *Giselle*, I heard nothing but the rasp and clatter of merry-makers' cars taking off in the small hours of the morning.

Another delightful factor was the fog.

All day it thickened stealthily outside, though at first, I did not waste a glance on it. When dusk approached, however, and the time came to leave for the Old Vic, it assumed menacing proportions. Not content with being an ordinary specimen, it congealed with yellow relish into what Charles Dickens called 'A London Particular'. All too well I remembered that a fog had tried to prevent me from joining the Diaghilev Ballet, a pea-souper which enveloped Victoria Station in 1925! I had given it the slip at last, but here was another, threatening to cut me off from Giselle. I would not allow it to do this, of course, even though I had to grope my way to the tube station, feeling for railings and kerbstones, instead of driving off in a taxi, ballerina-style. But I had a horrible feeling it would cut off the audience!

However, this miraculously was not so. During the first short ballet, I learned that the theatre was filling up. I was further cheered by a gift package, sent round before the performance by Marie Rambert, who was in the audience. This contained the white bodice worn by Tamara Karsavina in Act Two of the Diaghilev *Giselle*. Today I still prize it in my 'Giselle Collection', and it shares a place of honour with a shoe worn by Spessivtzeva at her last performance in London.

Of my own first performance, I confess I remember little in detail. I was mainly preoccupied with trying to keep calm and have my wits about me! All went smoothly—so I learned from the morning papers. Giselle must have come out of her cottage door, have seen the bright morning, met her lover, whom she knows only as Loys, and danced the joyous dances of the vintage. The disclosure that Loys is Count Albrecht and cannot marry her, must have come in due course. Hilarion, the jealous woodcutter, produced his tell-tale evidence, Princess Bathilde appeared to claim her betrothed; poor Giselle's mind snapped, and she began the broken dance which ends in death. . . . Obviously all

160

this happened on the night of January 1st, 1934! But I do remember that the fog began to seep into the theatre during Act One. By Act Two, when Giselle is a spirit, it had really arrived, and affected our breathing somewhat. . . . As members of the audience afterwards remarked, no producer could have improved on this forest of authentic mist! But here again, I can only assume that my Giselle danced her ghostly dances with Albrecht, pleaded for his life with the Wili Queen, and saved him at last, only to return to her grave as dawn flushed gold through the dark forest. . . . I know there were wonderful flowers afterwards, and famous dancers and personalities came to my dressing-room. But I cannot even remember if there was a party!

Alicia Markova
Giselle and I, 1960

The flowering of British ballet in the past fifty years is due in large part to the tireless efforts expended by two extraordinary women, Ninette de Valois and Marie Rambert. Her interest in dance sparked by a performance by Isadora Duncan, Rambert became a student of Jaques-Dalcroze and was subsequently chosen by Sergei Diaghilev to instruct members of the Ballets Russes in the Dalcroze method. In this case the lessons may have been more important for the teacher than her students, for exposure to the ballet world caused Rambert to give up her work with Dalcroze and enroll in the classes of Enrico Cecchetti, instructor of the Diaghilev company. It was there that Rambert met and began to work with the legendary Nijinsky.

I wore proper ballet shoes and did a hard class every day as well as a practice on my own. In this Nijinsky helped me quite often by explaining details to me entirely in his own way. Explaining is the wrong word when applied to Nijinsky. He spoke very little, and words did not come easily to him, which is why the rehearsing of his ballets always took so long. But he demonstrated the details of the movement so clearly and perfectly that it left no doubt as to the way it had to be done. He had such a high arch and such strength and suppleness of foot that the sole of one foot could clasp the back of the ankle of the other as though it were a hand (in the position *sur le cou de pied*). In addition to the class every morning which we all did, he used to do all the exercises again, this time partly made up, in preparation for the performance. Of course, I never failed to watch that.

One is often asked whether his jump was really as high as it is always described. To that I answer: 'I don't know how far from the ground it was, but I know it was near the stars.' Who would watch the floor when he danced? He transported you at once into higher spheres with the sheer ecstasy of his flight.

The most absurd theories were put forward about his anatomy. People said that the bones in his feet were like a bird's—as though a bird flew because of its feet! But, in fact, he *did* have an exceptionally long Achilles tendon which allowed him, with his heels firmly on the ground and the back upright, to bend the knees to the utmost before taking a spring, and he had powerful thighs. As to his famous poising in the air, he indeed created the illusion of it by the ecstasy of his expression at the apex of the leap, so that *this* unique moment penetrated into every spectator's consciousness, and seemed to last. His landing, from whatever height he jumped, was like a cat's. He had that unique touch of the foot on the ground which can only be compared to the pianist's touch of the fingers on the keys. It was as subtle and as varied.

And then there was his unique interpretation. He wafted the perfume of the rose in *Spectre de la Rose*; he was the very spirit of Chopin in *Les Sylphides*; he looked like a Hamlet in *Giselle*; his Petrushka broke your heart with his sorrow, and his Faune had the real breath of antiquity.

As to his choreography, I would not hesitate to affirm that it was he, more than anyone else, who revolutionised the classical ballet and was fifty years ahead of his time. Fokine was a logical development of Petipa, but Nijinsky introduced completely new principles. He produced three ballets in all: *l'Après-Midi d'un Faune*, *Jeux* and *Sacre du Printemps*. For each of them he established a basic position strictly adhered to all through the ballet. For *Faune* he took his inspiration from Greek vases and bas-reliefs. The body was facing front while the head and feet were always seen in profile. The deportment had to be classical, yet the head had independent movements not connected with deportment in the classical vocabulary, and so had the arms. It was an orchestration of the body, with each part playing a totally different melody. There was nothing you could do automatically. The walking was all done on one line parallel to the footlights, the whole foot on the ground. It was an incredibly difficult position to achieve, let alone use in walking, or changing direction, or combining with highly stylised arm movements. He did not explain why he wanted them thus, but he showed again and again the way they had to be done until he obtained a perfect copy of his own movement. His method of creation was diametrically opposed to Fokine's. Fokine always took the dancers into his confidence and allowed them, even encouraged them, to participate in the creation of a character. Not so Nijinsky. When once I was extolling the virtues of *Petrushka* to him, saying it was Fokine's masterpiece, he said that it *was* so, as far as the three main characters went, but the crowd was treated too loosely, and everybody did what they wanted within the space indicated to them. Nijinsky on the contrary did not allow the slightest freedom of movement or gesture and exacted only a perfect copy. No wonder it took some hundred and twenty rehearsals for *l'Après-midi d'un Faune*, lasting about ten minutes, to be achieved as he wished, since not a single movement could be done spontaneously, each limb having to be studied separately. He required a perfect ballet technique and then broke it down consciously to his own purpose—and then it proved a masterpiece. Each nymph looked a goddess. Although they were incapable of understanding Nijinsky's intentions, the mere fact of faithfully copying his unique movements gave them the requisite style. He told them: no expression in the face, you must just be as though asleep with your eyes open—like statues. . . .

It was the painter Roerich who first suggested the subject of *Sacre du Printemps*. He then worked on the theme with Diaghilev, Stravinsky and Nijinsky. It was to be prehistoric Russia and represent the rites of spring. Stravinsky had finished his magnificent score by 1912, and we started the rehearsals with the company that same year.

Nijinsky again first of all established the basic position: feet very turned in, knees slightly bent, arms held in reverse of the classical position, a primitive, prehistoric posture. The steps were very simple: walking smoothly or stamping, jumps mostly off both feet, landing heavily. There was only one a little more complicated dance for the maidens in the first scene. It was mostly done in groups, and each group has its own precise rhythm to follow. In the dance (if one can call it that) of the Wisest Elder, he walked two steps against every three steps of the ensemble. In the second scene the dance of the sacrifice of the Chosen Virgin was powerful and deeply moving. I watched Nijinsky again and again teaching it to Maria Piltz. Her reproduction was very pale by comparison with his ecstatic performance, which was the greatest tragic dance I have ever seen.

The first night of that ballet was the most astonishing event. Already the music of *Petrushka* had provoked the absolute hatred of the Vienna orchestra when we danced there in 1912. At rehearsal they threw down their bows in fury and called it 'Schweinerei'. Diaghilev went down into the pit and argued with them for quite a while before they consented to play—and then they sabotaged it.

And now in Paris in 1913 at the first sounds of the music, shouts and hissing started in the audience, and it was very difficult for us on the stage to hear the music, the more so as part of the audience began to applaud in an attempt to drown the hissing. We all desperately tried to keep time without being able to hear the rhythm clearly. In the wings Nijinsky counted the bars to guide us. . . .

But after the interlude things became even worse, and during the sacrificial dance real pandemonium broke out. That scene began with Maria Piltz, the Chosen Virgin, standing on the spot trembling for many bars, her folded hands under her right cheek, her feet turned in, a truly prehistoric and beautiful pose. But to the audience of the time it appeared ugly and comical.

A shout went up in the gallery:

'Un docteur!'

Somebody else shouted louder:

'Un dentiste!'

Then someone else screamed:

'Deux dentistes!'

And so it went on. One elegant lady leaned out of her box and slapped a man who was clapping. But the performance went on to the end.

MARIE RAMBERT
Quicksilver, 1972

In the mind of the general public, the career of Anna Pavlova stands as a testament to the drive for perfection in classical ballet. The Russian-born dancer reached the position of prima ballerina *at the Maryinsky Theater in St. Petersburg before beginning the peripatetic life that brought her art to such far-flung locations as China, Egypt, Argentina, and virtually every country in Europe. Pavlova's influence was especially strong in developing a ballet audience in the United States, as her manager and close friend Sol Hurok recalled in his memoirs.*

In 1916, [Charles B.] Dillingham engaged Pavlova to appear at the Hippodrome, with her partner, Alexandre Volinine....

Every night I was there in my favorite place at the back of the house. I soon learned the time schedule. I could manage to miss the skaters, the jugglers, the "mammoth" minstrels, the acrobats, the jumbo elephants. I would arrive a few minutes before Pavlova's entrance. I watched and worshipped from afar. I had never met her. "Who was I," I asked myself, "to meet a divinity?"

One night, as the falling curtain cut her off from my view, a hand fell on my shoulder. It was Dillingham. . . . He looked at me with a little smile and said, "Come along, Sol. I'm going back to her dressing-room."

The long hoped for but never really expected moment had come. Long had I rehearsed the speech I should make when and if this moment ever arrived. Now the time was here and I was dumb. I could only look.

The Swan extended her hand as Dillingham presented me. She smiled. I bent low over the world's most expressive hand. At her suggestion the three of us went to supper in the Palisades Amusement Park outdoor restaurant, overlooking the Hudson and upper Manhattan.

I shall have a few things to say about Pavlova, the artist, about Pavlova, the *ballerina*. Perhaps even more important is Pavlova, the woman, Pavlova, the human being. These qualities came tumbling forth at our first meeting. The impression was ineradicable. As she ate a prodigious steak, as she laughed and talked, here was a sure and certain indication of her insatiable love of life and its good things. . . .

Anna Pavlova was a firm believer in the "star" system, firmly entrenched as she was in the unassailable position of the *prima ballerina assoluta*. Her companies were always adequate. They were completely and perfectly disciplined. They were at all times reflections of her own directing and organizing ability. Always there were supporting dancers of more than competence. Her partners are names to be honored and remembered in ballet: Adolph Bolm, . . . Mikhail Mordkin, Laurent Novikoff, Alexandre Volinine, and Pierre Vladimiroff. . . .

In its time and place her repertoire was large and varied. Pavlova was acquainting a great country with an art hitherto unknown. She was bringing ballet to the masses. If there was more convention than experiment in her programmes, it must be remembered that there did not exist an audience even for convention, much less one ready for experimentation. An audience had to be created. . . .

. . . Pavlova never indulged in exhibitions of technical feats of remarkable virtuosity for the mere sake of eliciting gasps from an audience. Hers was an exhibition of the traditional school at its best, a school famed for its soundness. Her balance was something almost incredible; but never was it used for circus effects. There was in everything she did an exquisite lyricism, and an incomparable grace. . . . Diaghileff, with whom her independent, individualistic spirit could remain only a brief time, called her " . . . the greatest *ballerina* in the world. Like a Taglioni, she doesn't dance, but floats; of her, also, one might say she could walk over a cornfield without breaking a stalk." . . .

. . . Hers was a highly personal art. The purity and nobility of her style compensated and more than compensated for any production shortcomings. The important thing she left behind is an ineffable spirit that inhabits every performance of classical ballet, every classroom where classical ballet is taught.

SOL HUROK
S. Hurok Presents, 1953

It is usually left for historians or scholars to isolate the social forces that cause a certain movement to flourish at one time or another. In the case of modern dance, our understanding can be enriched by the observations of those artists who shaped its growth during the first half of the twentieth century—in particular the words of that seminal figure in the dance world, Martha Graham.

Throughout time dance has not changed in one essential function. The function of the dance is communication. The responsibility that dance fulfill its function belongs to us who are dancing today.

To understand dance for what it is, it is necessary we know from whence it comes and where it goes. It comes from the depths of man's inner nature, the unconscious, where memory dwells. As such it inhabits the dancer. It goes into the experience of man, the spectator, awakening similar memories.

Art is the evocation of man's inner nature. Through art, which finds its roots in man's unconscious—race memory—is the history and psyche of race brought into focus.

We are making a transition from 18th to 20th century thinking. A new vitality is possessing us. Certain depths of the intellect are being explored. Great art never ignores human values. Therein lies its roots. This is why forms change.

No art can live and pass untouched through such a vital period as we are now experiencing. Man is discovering himself as a world.

All action springs from necessity. This necessity is called by various names: inspiration, motivation, vision, genius. There is a difference of inspiration in the dance today.

Once we strove to imitate gods—we did god dances. Then we strove to become part of nature by representing natural forces in dance forms—winds—flowers—trees.

Dance was no longer performing its function of communication. By communication is not meant to tell a story or to project an idea, but to communicate experience by means of action and perceived by action. We were not speaking to that insight in man which would elevate him to a new strength through an heightened sense of awareness. Change had already taken place in man, was already in his life manifestations. While the arts do not create change, they register change.

This is the reason for the appearance of the modern dance. The departure of the dance from classical and romantic delineations was not an end in itself, but the means to an end. It was not done perversely to dramatize ugliness, or to strike at sacred tradition—to destroy from sheer inability to become proficient in the technical demands of a classical art. The old forms could not give voice to the more fully awakened man. They had to undergo metamorphosis—in some cases destruction, to serve as a medium for a time differently organized. . . .

I refuse to admit that the dance has limitations that prevent its acceptance and understanding—or that the intrinsic purity of the art itself need be touched. The reality of the dance is its truth to our inner life. Therein lies its power to move and communicate experience. The reality of dance can be brought into focus—that is into the realm of human values—by simple, direct, objective means. We are a visually stimulated world today. The eye is not to be denied. Dance need not change—it has only to stand revealed.

MARTHA GRAHAM
Remarks, 1937

The palpable air of mystery and adventure that has always surrounded Martha Graham and her company evolved from a combination of Graham's superhuman dedication to her work and keen sense of privacy. Often misunderstood or misjudged by the press, Graham usually kept the news media at arm's length. But in 1947 a writer for The New Yorker, *Angelica Gibbs, received an opportunity to observe and interview Graham and her co-workers, and the resulting profile remains one of the finest evocations of the Graham persona in print.*

Most professional dancers agree that Miss Graham is without equal—"the absolute frontier," as Agnes de Mille, one of her few close friends, puts it. Even ballet people, usually a carping lot when it comes to appraising the work of rivals and especially the work of rivals in the rival camp, have been known to concede that she has given them a greater understanding of the potentialities of their own medium. . . . In several universities and colleges where she makes appearances when she is on the road, she is now considered, in the words of one professor of dancing, "completely compulsory." . . .

. . . A friendly, soft-spoken, businesslike woman in her late forties, given to wearing the kind of tailored gray wool suit commonly associated with prosperous feminine executives, she has a way with people that her admirers speak of reverently as "the Graham spell". . . . "Naturally, I realize in my more lucid moments that Martha may possibly be a little lower than the angels," a young composer said not long ago. "But I always forget it again when I'm in her presence." . . .

Miss Graham is of medium height, slim, loose-limbed, dark-haired, and, by conventional, or Conover, standards, not at all beautiful. . . . Because Miss Graham's expression while dancing has always been conspicuously deadpan (it took her ten years to key herself up to the point of displaying a smile onstage), her extremities have undergone closer inspection by the public than her face. In the middle nineteen-thirties, when her hands began, in the jargon of the critics, to "evolve"—that is, to unclench a bit—both the *Times* and the *Christian Science Monitor* devoted several columns of rapturous comment to the phenomenon. . . . As for Miss Graham's feet, they are, as a young lady once remarked during one of those intense anatomical discussions dear to dancers, not exactly classical in their proportions but extremely interesting, nonetheless. "They're little, nutlike feet," she explained, glowing. What many consider the definitive comment on Miss Graham's feet, however, was made a decade or so ago by a clubwoman in Richmond, Virginia, where the dancer was performing. Leaving her seat in the middle of a Graham solo, the woman traipsed hopefully down the aisle, and, after adjusting her pince-nez the better to inspect the dancer's bare left foot, which was protruding from the folds of a sackcloth costume, muttered audibly, "Only *five* toes, for pity's sake!" Then she stalked back to her seat again, downcast and grumpy. . . .

. . . When she [Miss Graham] reflects upon all the critical double-talk to which she has been subjected during her career, she becomes more convinced than ever that language is hopelessly inadequate as a means of expression and that she can best prove it by going right on dancing out her ideas. "After all," she said recently, "the primary bond between people is undoubtedly physical, since the body is the one thing we all have in common. Our job now is to get our message to the greatest number of people in the shortest possible time." . . .

Miss Graham's symbolic, or metaphorical, use of language seems to work best when she employs it to explain her conception of a dance to the composer she has commissioned to write its score. She prefers to sit down with him and talk over her ideas, but often she has to do it all by mail. When, for example, in 1941, Aaron Copland, who was attending to some Hollywood chores, was also composing the music for Miss Graham's "Appalachian Spring," a dance concerned with the westward pioneer movement, he received several spirited letters of guidance written by Miss Graham at obviously feverish speed and in the style she employs when talking things over. One of her proposals had to do with suggesting the thoughts of a pioneer mother when she sees an Indian girl on whose parents' land the frontiersmen had settled. . . . Copland got the idea perfectly and set to work. As things turned out, the Indian Girl didn't actually appear in the production, because Miss Graham decided that the idea she had in mind was adequately conveyed by other means. This method of collaboration, though, has since been proved successful, for "Appalachian Spring," all of which was worked out in the same manner, is acknowledged to be one of Miss Graham's most effective pieces, and Copland's score won a Pulitzer Prize. . . .

In normal times—that is, when Miss Graham isn't involved in a production—the atmosphere in the studio is rather like that of a pleasant progressive school. The students call their headmistress by her first name and wait hopefully for an opportunity to tell her their troubles, which range from aching metatarsals to broken hearts. When rehearsals begin, tension increases rapidly. During the last week before a production is ready, the scene is chaotic indeed. The reception room is packed every afternoon with importunate people: the production's composer, say, who, after handing in his score two months late, wants it back to make a few major revisions; a professor of the dance from a Midwestern university; Mr. Hudelson [Graham's manager], with a reporter in tow; a New York University coed, a student at the Graham School, who has just returned from Wanamaker's with some more material for costumes; a prospective pupil from Hollywood; and four women from God only knows where, who have dropped in mostly to tell Miss Graham that they think she's wonderful. Sitting at a desk in one corner of the room is Robert Schnitzer, who is secretary of the school and whose duties consist largely of trying to placate everyone at once. There may also be half a dozen feminine members of the company, some seated on the floor and some on a bench that flanks one wall, as they sew away on their costumes and chat with Mr. Horst [the musical director], who, white-haired, corpulent, and calm, is sipping a glass of elderberry wine. From the rehearsal room come muffled snatches of dissonance, musical and oral. Presently, the door opens and several perspiring, barefoot dancers totter out. Miss Graham, in a long, black robe, appears for an instant behind them, glances Medea-like at the strangers, and then closes the door on the whole bunch with a good deal of emphasis. Mr. Schnitzer and Mr. Hudelson raise their eyebrows in a gesture of helplessness. The four women of uncertain origin get together to discuss whether each saw what the others saw and whether it was the real thing. The members of the company go on sewing industriously, but through the ranks, between sighs of admiration, runs the well-worn tribute "Martha's terrific today!"

ANGELICA GIBBS
The New Yorker, 1947

Modern ballet audiences owe an enormous debt to Sergei Diaghilev and the company he organized in Paris in 1909, the Ballets Russes. Diaghilev brought together the cream of Russian dancers and choreographers and many of the most creative new craftsmen in music and art. The dances that resulted from their collaborations fundamentally altered the direction of ballet's evolution. In the midst of this highly charged atmosphere two figures dominated all the others, Diaghilev and his most favored protégé, Vaslav Nijinsky, as can be seen in the memoirs of Diaghilev dancer Lydia Sokolova.

When I joined the ballet in April, 1913, Nijinsky was sole *maître de ballet*. His *Faune* was in the current repertory; his *Jeux* and *Sacre* were in rehearsal, and Diaghilev must have been happy watching over the birth, however difficult, of the new experimental works. There was every reason to believe that the company would continue with the divine Nijinsky as principal dancer and the rather less divine Nijinsky as choreographer for many years to come.

In appearance Nijinsky was himself like a faun—a wild creature who had been trapped by society and was always ill at ease. When addressed, he turned his head furtively, looking as if he might suddenly butt you in the stomach. He moved on the balls of his feet, and his nervous energy found an outlet in fidgeting: when he sat down he twisted his fingers or played with his shoes. He hardly spoke to anyone, and seemed to exist on a different plane. Before dancing he was even more withdrawn, like a bewitched soul. I used to watch him practising his wonderful jumps in the first position, flickering his hands; I had never seen anyone like him before.

When Diaghilev came for the first time to one of our rehearsals I was scared stiff. His presence was awe-inspiring and he radiated self-assurance, like royalty. Tall and heavy, with a little moustache and a monocle, he advanced into the room, followed by a group of friends. Everyone who was seated stood up, and silence fell. With [ballet master] Grigoriev following discreetly a yard or two behind, he passed through the crowd of dancers, stopping here and there to exchange a greeting. Any male dancer to whom he spoke would click his heels together and bow.

Diaghilev then sat down, and we three English girls were summoned before him. Cowed by his majestic personality, I felt like a naughty school-child. Mim Rambert came to our rescue and translated his words. He told us that we should have to work very hard to improve our standard of dancing, and that we must take great care to do everything Maestro Cecchetti told us. We were glad when the time came for us to lose ourselves once more in the crowd. Diaghilev spoke quietly and deliberately, and during all the years I knew him I seldom heard him raise his voice.

At the start of our season when we were assembled on the stage before the performance, Diaghilev would wander on, looking magnificent in tails. He knew his appearance was impressive and he behaved accordingly. He would look for creases in the scenery, make sure the lighting was correct, mumble a few words to Nijinsky or Karsavina, ignoring the rest of us, give Grigoriev the word to begin, and go through the pass door into the front of the house. Carefully shaved and scented, his hair touched up with black dye, except for a white streak left on one side, he looked incredibly distinguished and I felt proud to have him as my director. This feeling of pride in Diaghilev never left me in later years, even when I knew he had holes in the soles of his shoes. Yet grand as he was, we always addressed him in the Russian fashion by his own first name and his father's, 'Sergei Pavlovitch'.

LYDIA SOKOLOVA
Dancing for Diaghilev, 1960

Among the world's leading ballet companies, the New York City Ballet occupies an unusual position. Its aesthetic profile is the reflection of one man, George Balanchine, the company's founder and artistic director and, in the opinion of many, the finest choreographer of the present era. But even for the greatest of talents, setting a new ballet requires exhausting, repetitive work, as the ballet critic Edwin Denby observed during the preparation of a new work entitled Variants.

Making a ballet takes an unbounded patience from everybody concerned. An outsider is fascinated to be let in on the minuteness of the workmanship. But then he finds no way out of that minuteness. Listening to the same few bars pounded again and again on the piano, watching the same movements started at top speed and broken off, again and again, the fascinated outsider after two hours and a half of that finds himself going stir crazy. Seeing a ballet in the theatre the momentum of action and music carries the audience into a world of zest and grandeur. In performance the dancers look ravishing. In rehearsal they look like exhausted champions attempting Mt. Everest, knowing how limited the time is, step by step, hold by hold, roped together by the music, with the peak nowhere in sight. . . .

Variants was rehearsed during the ballet season, when the dancers, in addition to performance and class, have repertory rehearsals as well; union rules specified the hours available. Besides inventing his ballet at such hours, Balanchine also had every morning and evening decisive responsibilities in running the company and planning its future.

Between September and November, he had made four new pieces. The first, to the most recent Stravinsky score, was followed by a ballet to Donizetti music; then he presented an hour-long ballet set to two song cycles by Brahms, and called *Liebeslieder Walzer*. *Liebeslieder Walzer*—with a cast of eight—turned out to be a masterpiece, glorious and magical. No other choreographer, no other company could have done it, but one isn't aware of that, the poetry of it—the secret image —is so absorbing. Two weeks after *Liebeslieder* he presented *Ragtime*, a duet witty and deceptively elementary in the way the Stravinsky score is. Six days after *Ragtime*, he began *Variants*.

Balanchine usually prepares a ballet far in advance. He has said that he prepares for a long time by playing and studying the score—"I listen, listen, listen, listen." On the other hand, he does not look for steps until the actual performers are with him in the rehearsal studio.

Variants had been commissioned at his request. Like some of [Gunther] Schuller's previous music, it was to be in Third Stream style, scored for the Modern Jazz Quartet and symphonic orchestra. The choice implied a Third-Stream-type ballet, a non-existent species. Balanchine prepared for it by listening to jazz albums. He didn't study the score during the summer lay-off while he was growing roses, because until September Schuller was too busy to begin writing it. The last installment of the piano version was delivered in November.

The composer's plan—a suite—featured the Jazz Quartet artists singly and jointly accompanied by small orchestral groups; the introduction was for full orchestra, the conclusion for full orchestra plus Quartet. The choreographer's plan was a dance suite. He wanted half the cast—two solo boys and eight ensemble girls—to be Negroes; but the girls weren't found. He picked his dancers, cast each of the dance numbers, decided which numbers to make first. At that point the first rehearsal sheet was posted; the date for opening night confirmed.

At the start of the first rehearsal he chose a way of working which he kept until the whole piece had been created. At every point he took each role. The process looked like this. Standing near the dancer, he signaled the pianist to play ahead, and clapped his hands when he wanted him to break off. The pianist repeated the fragment once or twice while Balanchine listened intently. Then without music, he took the position in which the dancer would have to start, and stood absorbed, sometimes turning his head very slightly in this direction or that, sometimes slightly moving on his feet. He was inventing the next figure. He seemed to test the feel of it, and decide. That done, he glanced at the dancer, stressed the starting position, and without music showed the move. The first time he showed it, he did it from start to finish at full performance force and speed.

The dancers reproduced it, adding to it at once—in ballet style—the full extension of the body, the turn-out of legs and feet, the toe-step or leap he had merely implied. A nondancer might have wondered how they could guess so much; but they seemed to guess right almost always. As expert dancers they were following out the logical balletic consequences of the main move he had shown. Sometimes they asked about a detail left in doubt, and he specified the answer in ballet terminology.

Moving at the speed and force he had shown, the fully extended bodies of the dancers sometimes developed a sudden momentum that was scary. But the jet of it took the dancer to the right spot at the right instant. The impetus came from eccentric swings from the shoulder or waist, the support from handholds. When the choreographer first showed such a move, he literally threw himself into it, and let his feet take care of themselves. When the dancers couldn't manage the move, he repeated it. Between them they tracked down the trouble to a change of hand, a specific angle or stance, or an extra step which he had taken instinctively, and which the dancers had overlooked.

Soon, when he made such a move the first time, he repeated it at once, stressing how the feet stepped and the hands reached for support. At the second rehearsal, he spent more than a half hour on a fantastic sequence lasting a few bars that wouldn't work to counts; after that whatever took too long to learn he discarded before it was set by counts to the music. (Had he been making a piece in regulation ballet steps to music easy to remember by ear, the process would have been far less cumbersome.)

Balanchine's care was for the mechanics of momentum. He did not mention expression. Watching him do a move full force, an outsider might often have been struck by his expression in it—a quality of gesture which was directly to the point. It was beautiful. The dancers did not imitate that. Their expression when it appeared was their own, and he did not criticize it. Expression seemed to be treated as a Jeffersonian inalienable right. And perhaps it is.

Later rehearsals were moved to the theatre building, to a gloomy echoing room upstairs modeled on a chapter-room in a castle of the Knights Templar. Here Balanchine took the dancers by shifts and choreographed from ten thirty to six. "I work like a dentist," he remarked. He sometimes looked exhausted, but a joke revived him. When dancers lost the count, he did not nag or look depressed. The phrases he made for the chorus were easy motions, but their peculiar timing required exact counts. He kept checking the counts in the score. During ten minute or half hour breaks, he stayed alone in the rehearsal room, rereading the score, playing it, checking on the metronome speed. The composer who was to conduct the ballet watched a rehearsal, and Balanchine brought up the metronome speed; he referred to the metronome speed given in the score: Schuller, experienced with orchestras but not with Balanchine choreography, evaded his insistence. Solo rehearsals, chorus rehearsals, stage rehearsals, orchestra rehearsals, dress rehearsals, lighting rehearsals.

The first orchestra rehearsal for the dancers came the day before opening. The dancers had become used to recognizing landmarks or cues in the piano score. The colorful orchestration obliterated these. But they had expected as much. Since they had memorized the score by counts, they could perform to the measure whatever unforeseen noises the orchestra made. Disaster threatened nevertheless. Finding the music difficult, the instrumentalists slowed down; but the dancers rushing headlong couldn't slow down without toppling. The momentum of their off-balance rushes worked at a specific speed that had been agreed on between composer and choreographer and fixed by metronome. The dancers had to rely on it and now it turned unreliable. The choreographer's well-known coolness adjusted what was possible. And suddenly the first night's performance was over. There was polite applause.

EDWIN DENBY
Dancers, Buildings and People in the Streets, 1965

To a large degree modern dance has been the product of the creative drive of American dancers. One major exception is the work of the German-born dancer and choreographer Mary Wigman. A student of Emile Jaques-Dalcroze and Rudolf van Laban in the early part of her career, Wigman developed a singular approach to dance movement that has influenced dancers both in Europe and the United States. The essense of her artistic credo is contained in the thoughtfully written essay, "The Language of Dance."

The dance is a living language which speaks of man—an artistic message soaring above the ground of reality in order to speak, on a higher level, in images and allegories of man's innermost emotions and need for communication. It might very well be that, above all, the dance asks for direct communication without any detours. Because its bearer and intermediary is man himself, and because his instrument of expression is the human body, whose natural movement forms the material for the dance, the only material which is his own and his own to use. This is why the dance and its expression are so exclusively bound to man and his ability to move. Where this ability ceases to be, the dance faces the limitations of its creative and performing possibilities.

This seems so little! And yet in this littleness lies the language of the dance in all its manifold forms which can be changed anew time and again. Certainly, bodily movement alone is not yet dance. But it is the elemental and incontestable basis without which there would be no dance. When the emotion of the dancing man frees the impulse to make visible his yet invisible images, then it is through bodily movement that these images manifest themselves in their first stages. And it is movement through which the projected dance gesture receives the living breath of its rhythmically pulsating power....

The same way as music, dance too is called an "art of time." This holds true as long as one refers to the measurable, countable rhythmic passages which can be controlled in time. But that's not all! It would be little else but stale theory were we to determine the rhythm of the dance solely from the element of time. True, counting is spelled with capital letters by us dancers. We need it especially in our choreographic work, during the process of creation and the rehearsing of group works in the modern dance or ballet. We need it as an expediency to account for the structure of the two cooperating artistic languages, dance and music, to attune them to each other in their temporal course and bring them together in harmonious understanding. We need it to define the beats, to clarify the transitions from one theme to the next, to be precise in giving the necessary accents, the moments of arrested movement and breathing. There is always counting. The musicians count and the dancers count. And sometimes they miss one another in counting, because the musicians count along the musical line whereas the dancers arrive at their counting through the rhythm of movement.

In the same manner as time, if not even more compellingly, the element of strength plays its part in the dance—the dynamic force, moving and being moved, which is the pulsebeat of the life of dance. One could also call it the living breath of dancing. For breath is the mysterious great master who reigns unknown and unnamed behind all and everything—who silently commands the function of muscles and joints—who knows how to fire with passion and to relax, how to whip up and to restrain—who puts the breaks in the rhythmic structure and dictates the phrasing of the flowing passages—who, above and beyond all this, regulates the temper of expression in its interplay with the colorfulness of rhythm and melody. Of course, this has nothing in common with a normal breathing method. The dancer must be able to breathe in every one of his stances and situations. He is then hardly aware of his organic breathing; he is ruled by the law of his dynamically propelled power of breathing which reveals itself in the momentary degree of its intensity and strain. When the dancer crosses through space with solemnly measured steps, his deep and calm breathing gives his carriage and movement an appearance of innermost composure and completion in itself; and when—by incessantly springing up and down—he throws himself into a condition of flickering agitation which not only takes possession of his body but of the entire being, then there no longer exists a moment of quiet breathing for him. He breathes, rather, with the same vibration that fills and shakes his whole being.

There is hardly another dance movement in which the power of dynamic breathing, increasing effect and accomplishment, is felt as strongly as in the leap. When the dancer starts to jump, he chases the stream of his breath like lightning from below to the top, from the feet upward through the body, to be able to hold his breath from the instant of leaving the ground until he has reached the height of his leap and has almost gone beyond it. In these few seconds of his utmost exertion, holding his breath, he actually defies all gravity, becomes a creature of the air, and seems to fly or float through space. At the downcurve only, his breath flows back into the relaxing body and returns the dancer to the earth after his short soaring flight.

Time, strength, and space: these are the elements which give the dance its life. Of this trinity of elemental powers, it is space which is the realm of the dancer's real activity, which belongs to him because he himself creates it. It is not the tangible, limited, and limiting space of concrete reality, but the imaginary, irrational space of the danced dimension, that space which can erase the boundaries of all corporeality and can turn the gesture, flowing as it is, into an image of seeming endlessness, losing itself in self-completion like rays, like streams, like breath. Height and depth, width and breadth, forward, sideward, and backward, the horizontal and the diagonal—these are not only technical terms or theoretical notions for the dancer. After all, he experiences them in his own body. And they become his living experience because through them he celebrates his union with space. Only in its spatial embrace can the dance achieve its final and decisive effect. Only then the fleeting signs are compressed into a legible and lasting mirror image in which the message of the dance grows into what it should and must be: language—the living, artistic language of dance.

And now let's lower our voice and be a bit wary! For we want to enter the realm of creativity, the space in which the hidden form and the seeking form circle one another, intertwine and wait in the twilight of their dream for the light to come in order to give them color and contours and to illuminate what has turned into an "image." Whoever would be brash enough to enter here with the blazing torch of curiosity would find little more than a mistily drifting cluster of images. For this space does not permit a direct approach. It does not respond to concrete demands. It does not yet know of structure, it knows neither name nor number. It does not want to yield to anything, it does not heed commands. It is the space of creative readiness and is a sanctuary. Therefore, let us lower our voice and listen to the pulsebeat of our heart, to the whisper and murmur of our own blood, which is the sound of this space. This sound wants to become song! But its wings are still tied, it lacks the strength to unfold them and to speak in its upward flight. Thus it sinks back into the space of twilight depth, sucks in its own powers, and returns, heavy with dreams and images, into the realm in which it may be comprehended and may yield to form.

Creative ability belongs to the sphere of reality as much as to the realm of fantasy. And there are always two currents, two circles of tension, which magnetically attract one another, flash up and oscillate together until, completely attuned, they penetrate one another: on the one hand, the creative readiness which evokes the image; on the other hand, the will to act whipped up to a point of obsession, that will which takes possession of the image and transforms its yet fleeting matter into malleable working substance in order to give it its final form in the crucible of molding.

MARY WIGMAN
"The Language of Dance," 1963

Agnes de Mille has distinguished herself as a choreographer in many different phases of the dance world: ballet, musical theater, and folk dancing. But no matter what type of stage her work is destined for, de Mille follows a well-tested approach to awaken her muse.

By the time I composed *Rodeo* I had crystallized a technique of composing. It was in essentials the same method I had fumbled with in my early pantomimes, but it has routined itself with the subsequent Broadway practice into a true discipline.

To make up a dance, I still need, as I needed then, a pot of tea, walking space, privacy and an idea. Although every piece I have done so far for a ballet company is a *ballet d'action* or story ballet, I have no preference for this type—quite the contrary—I think the lyric or abstract ballets more pleasing and much more enduring, but my knack has been for dramatics.

When I first visualize the dance, I see the characters moving in color and costume. Before I go into rehearsal, I know what costumes the people wear and generally what color and texture. I also, to a large extent, hear the orchestral effects....

I start sitting with my feet up and drinking pots of strong tea, but as I am taken into the subject I begin to move and before I know it I am walking the length of the studio and acting full out the gestures and scenes. The key dramatic scenes come this way. I never forget a single nuance of them afterwards; I do usually forget dance sequences.

The next step is to find the style of gesture. This is done standing and moving, again behind locked doors and again with a gramophone. Before I find how a character dances, I must know how he walks and stands. If I can discover the basic rhythms of his natural gesture, I will know how to expand them into dance movement.

It takes hours daily of blind instinctive moving and fumbling to find the revealing gesture, and the process goes on for weeks before I am ready to start composing. Nor can I think any of this out sitting down. My body does it for me. It happens. That is why the choreographic process is exhausting. It happens on one's feet after hours of work, and the energy required is roughly the equivalent of writing a novel and winning a tennis match simultaneously. This is the kernel, the nucleus of the dance. All the design develops from this.

Having established a scenario and discovered the style and key steps, I then sit down at my desk and work out the pattern of the dances. If the score is already composed, the dance pattern is naturally suggested by and derived from the pattern of the music. If it remains to be composed as it does in all musical comedies, the choreographer goes it alone. This, of course, is harder. Music has an enormous suggestive power and the design of the composer offers a helpful blueprint....

Through practice I have learned to project a whole composition in rough outline mentally and to know exactly how the dancers will look at any given moment moving in counterpoint in as many as five groups. As an aid in concentration, I make detailed diagrams and notes of my own arbitrary invention, intelligible only to me and only for about a week, but they are not comparable in exactness to music notation.

At this point, I am ready, God help me, to enter the rehearsal hall. . . .

Well, there they stand, the material of your craft, patient, disciplined, neat and hopeful in their black woolens. They will offer you their bodies for the next several weeks to milk the stuff of your ideas out of their muscles. They will submit to endless experimentation. They will find technique that has never been tried before; they will submerge their personalities and minds to the blindest, feeblest flutterings of yours. They will remember what you forget. They are pinning all the hopes of their past practices and future performings on the state of your brains. There they stand and consider you as you walk into the room. If they know you and are fond of you, it's easier. But at best, it's a soul-challenging moment. . . .

It's a good idea to give the company for a beginning something definite and technically difficult to get their feet down on. The minute they start to sweat they feel busy and useful. Like [Antony] Tudor, I always try to start with two or three dancers I know who are sympathetic to my suggestion, and I have learned to have the rehearsal planned through to the end, preferably on a piece of paper in case I dry up mentally. Standing and scratching one's head while the dancers cool off in their tights, and then put on extra sweaters, and then sit down on the floor, and then light cigarettes and start to talk, is what one wishes to avoid. No group of workers in the world is slower to lose faith or interest, but they are human. While you are struggling to find the exact phrasing they get tired in the back of their knees. And when you ask them to get off the floor and try the jump in the eighteenth variation they rise creaking. Then you grow hot with anger that you cannot solve the problem and punish their bodies for your own stupidity, forcing them to do it again and again and again, pretending that it is their lack of performance quality that invalidates the idea. But no one is fooled. Neither you nor they. You scold them. And your company quietly grows to hate you. They are now more or less useless for your purposes. If you were working with marble you could hack at it for a year without any deterioration of material. If you were writing a book you could lay down your pen, take a walk, take a nap, have some coffee and come back to find your manuscript just as you left it. But dancers stand with patient drawn faces waiting for your brains to click.

One could simply terminate a rehearsal and wait for a more fruitful moment. But after all, the dancers are there to work, the hall is rented, the pianist hired and attentive.

There are, however, the times when one scrapes absolute bottom. The manner in which he deals with these moments is the exact measure of a choreographer's experience. [George] Balanchine dismisses a rehearsal without any ado at all and goes home. If, on the other hand, he likes what he is doing, hell can break loose around him and he pays not the slightest mind. Short of hell he nearly always is surrounded by a roomful of chattering, knitting, practicing dancers and visitors. [Leonide] Massine holds the entire company in the room. They sit for hours sometimes while he wrestles with one or two soloists. If he gets stuck he keeps it to himself as he never explains a single thing he is doing to anyone he is working with. Martha Graham sends her group from the room and has it out with God. I cannot endure the sight of one person sitting down waiting. A sense of guilt and tedium oppresses me exactly as though I were failing a guest. I, therefore, allow in the room with me only the people I am working with, never any visitors, and inside the rehearsal room no one may sit down or chew gum or smoke. I have to keep myself geared to such a pitch that if I relax or allow the dancers to relax the rehearsal for all effective purposes is over. Outside in the waiting room or hall they may do as they like—drink, chew, eat, gossip, play cards. This pertains to the beginning weeks. When the composition stands by itself on the floor and is no longer a matter of hypnotism between me and the group, everything is easier.

But with all the good planning possible, there comes sooner or later the inevitable point of agony when the clock dictates and one must just set one's teeth and get on with it. Then one wrings the ultimate out of one's marrow. The astonishing fact is that it is there to be wrung.

The dancers themselves frequently help. For the very reason they are human and have wills and imaginations and styles of their own, their manner of moving will suggest an infinite number of ideas to the choreographer. They can evoke where clay and canvas cannot. The minute the choreographer moves a tentative hand or places a foot forward, they are behind him imitating. The stimulus of their interest will excite him. He will improvise beyond his expectations. He may not know exactly what he has done. But bright-eyes has seen; the gesture is immediately reproduced. The choreographer can then turn around and watch his idea on someone else's body. This he can correct and edit. A sensitive performer needs only a hint, a breath, and he is off, the rhythms generated in his body helping to push the design ahead. . . .

Sometimes the solo figures are developed first and the group patterns blocked in behind like the orchestration to a melody. Sometimes when the soloist has simple dramatic or storytelling movement the group is set first and the soloist added. In these cases I go to the back of the theater where I can get a perspective of the stage and add on the soloist by shouted direction. . . .

Big designs are largely headwork and must be visualized in advance. Obviously a large group is too disparate an instrument on which to improvise—until it is aroused.

Such times are memorable. They usually occur when the group is exhausted after hours of work, late in a studio at the dinner hour or at night in the theater when everyone else has gone home. There, in absolute privacy and with no impatience to be gone to other concerns, working together in perfect community of understanding, the moment comes. And quite simply every single performer knows what to do as though he were inside the composer's head. In this art, the interpreters are present at the actual moment of creation and if they share the labor they also know some of the glory. They are grateful for this and stand abashed and wondering. And so, by God, does the choreographer.

AGNES DE MILLE
Dance to the Piper, 1952

Illness forced Doris Humphrey to retire from dancing in 1945. Fortunately, she was able to continue her career as a choreographer and, as she demonstrates in remarks made to a class at the Juilliard School, pass on to young dancers her special insights into the art of making dances.

The choreographer is observant; he is not just interested in, but fascinated with all manifestations of form and shape. He notes the shapes of his environment, wherever he may be. In the city? He sees the architectural variations, the skyline, the tangled grotesqueries of water tanks, television wires, ventilators, the "feel" of the congestion, the preponderance of rectilinear lines, and the comedy of the small defiant brownstone squashed between two mammoth chromium and glass monsters. He sees the people, *en masse,* as in a street moving in kaleidoscopic patterns, or as individuals, old, middle-aged, young, who are meeting, parting, talking, walking, working. He is never bored when alone in public places; the world's people are always giving a show. He is also a close observer of people in more intimate situations; what movements do they make under the stress of various emotions: anger, affection, enthusiasm, boredom? If you would much rather think about your own personal problems, and find your greatest interest lies in perfecting a technique; if you have recurrent visions of yourself performing before vast audiences; or if you would like to have a job dancing in television and live comfortably—you are a potential or already-arrived dancer and not essentially a choreographer. As a dancer you have an entirely different set of problems, much more subjective, though fully as complicated as those of a choreographer.

The choreographer likes to discover and invent. He never ceases to be curious about the meaning of movement, and never stops wondering at the infinite possibilities and gradations of movement. The finding of a new sequence, or even a single gesture, has all the excitement of high adventure. He is acutely aware that other people differ from him physically and emotionally and he takes delight in discovering where their potentials lie, resisting the temptation to impose all his own idiosyncrasies on them.

And finally, the choreographer had better have something to say. This, to some young people, seems very formidable indeed and they immediately search their souls for grandiose or cosmic themes which are not only unnecessary but ill-advised. Leave the massive themes to the older heads and hands; they are difficult enough even for the veterans. All you really need is a genuine enthusiasm for something rather simple inspired by a subject you understand, an incident or a feeling in your own experience, music or poetry which will bear the added weight of dancing, a dramatic idea or a figure from history—there are many things to dance about. The important ingredient is your enthusiasm for it, plus its practicability: there are some things that cannot or should not be danced about. An apathetic approach, or a vague desire to be doing something is a good recipe for failure and, moreover, you need that initial excitement about the subject to tide you over the inevitable slump that besets all choreographers. . . .

And now a few words about the general position of the choreographer in the world of esthetics. You should always remember that the dance is the only art without a permanent record of itself, and I say this in spite of the fact that dance notation is making headway and that a few films have been made. In comparison to the durability of paintings, musical scores, books and sculpture, dance is highly perishable. It has a moth-like existence and dies in the spot-light. This means, among other things, that dancers do not have hundreds of scores from which to learn as musicians do, but must be in a place and a position to acquire any finished compositions from a live teacher or choreographer, from mouth to foot, so to speak. There must be thousands of young dancers with good technical equipment who, through various circumstances, have nothing to dance, or, worse than nothing, some trash thrown together in utter ignorance or desperation. The obvious answer to this is more choreographic information through notation, which is slow, or through more study of the subject at first hand, which is faster. If you, through me, can acquire some of the knowledge and skill you need in order to compose, you will be better equipped to deal with any situation in which you must depend on yourself. Suppose you were to wake up some morning to find that Fate had deposited you in a small town, any small town, or even a medium-sized city. The chances are that there would be no one who could teach you a good dance, nor any group you could join which had a knowledgeable director at its head. But you would not be at a loss completely because you would know something about choreography and could make dances of your own. They might not be masterpieces, but they could not be utterly without value. And one more thing I shall expect, wherever Fate may lead you: that you will spread the light of understanding among the people you meet, and do your bit to further the progress of the dance either as a teacher or a dancer or, best of all, as a choreographer.

Doris Humphrey
The Juilliard Review, 1956

A Chronology of Dance

Although the art of dance is as old as the human race, the Editors have begun this chronology in the sixteenth century because it is the earliest time that specific dance works can be attributed to individual artists.

Ballet Comique de la Reine, dance spectacle staged for Catherine de Médicis	1581	
	1582	Gregorian calendar introduced
*Publication of *Orchésographie*, a manual of ballroom dancing and deportment by Thoinot Arbeau	1588	English defeat Spanish Armada; Christopher Marlowe's *Dr. Faustus* performed
	1598	Edict of Nantes grants French Protestants equal political rights with Catholics
	1607	Performance of Monteverdi's *Orfeo*, considered the first opera
	1620	Pilgrims land at Plymouth Rock, Massachusetts
	1632	Galileo publishes experiments supporting Copernican theories on the solar system, and the following year is tried for heresy by the Inquisition
The raised stage of Richelieu's Palais Cardinal separates performers from audience	1636	Corneille writes the historical drama *Le Cid*
Salmacida Spolia, an English masque performed for King Charles I	1640	
	1643	Louis XIV succeeds to the throne of France
Louis XIV's first public dance performance	1651	Hobbes publishes *Leviathan*
Louis XIV portrays the Rising Sun in production entitled *Ballet de la Nuit*	1653	
Académie Royale de Danse founded by Louis XIV	1661	
Académie Royale de Musique founded	1669	Molière's *Tartuffe* performed after clerical ban against it is lifted
Premiere performance of Molière's *Le Bourgeois Gentilhomme*, a comedy featuring music and dance sequences	1670	
Louis XIV combines the Académie Royale de Danse and the Académie Royale de Musique	1672	
	1675	Sir Christopher Wren's masterpiece, St. Paul's, replaces an earlier cathedral destroyed in the Great Fire
First female dancers appear in Lully's ballet *Le Triomphe de l'Amour*	1681	
	1682	Peter the Great becomes tsar of Russia
Five fundamental foot positions come into general use	c.1700	
Opening of Paris Opéra Ballet School	1713	Signing of the Treaty of Utrecht provides for permanent separation of the thrones of Spain and France
John Weaver stages *The Loves of Mars and Venus*, first ballet without recitation or song, in London	1717	
	1721	Bach completes the six *Brandenburg Concertos*
Marie Sallé stages ballet version of Pygmalion fable, among the earliest choreography done by a woman	1734	
Presentation of Jean Philippe Rameau's spectacular opéra-ballet *Les Indes Galantes* in Paris	1735	
Jean Baptiste Landé founds St. Petersburg School of Ballet, forerunner of the Maryinsky Ballet Company	1738	John Wesley, founder of the Methodist Church, begins to preach in England

Jean Georges Noverre (1727-1810) wins acclaim following production of his ballet *Les Fêtes Chinoises* at Paris Opéra Comique	1754	
	1759	Publication of Voltaire's *Candide*
Publication of Noverre's *Letters on Dancing and Ballet*; Maryinsky Ballet becomes Imperial Russian Ballet	1760	
Gasparo Angiolini creates *Don Juan*, important early *ballet d'action*	1761	
	1762	Rousseau completes *The Social Contract*
	1785	*The Times* of London founded by John Walter
Vincenzo Galeotti stages *The Whims of Cupid and the Ballet Master* in Copenhagen; it remains a part of the repertory of the Royal Danish Ballet today	1786	
Jean Dauberval choreographs *La Fille Mal Gardée*, a comic ballet which has been restaged for presentation by Britain's Royal Ballet and American Ballet Theatre	1789	Parisians storm the Bastille; Declaration of the Rights of Man proclaimed
Charles Didelot's *Zephyr and Flora* features dancers lifted into the air with wires, giving the illusion of flight	1796	Edward Jenner uses first vaccine against smallpox
Charles Didelot, a Frenchman, named director of the Imperial Russian Ballet School	1801	Union of Great Britain and Ireland to form United Kingdom
	1804	Napoleon proclaimed emperor of France; Beethoven's *Eroica Symphony* given first performance
Techniques of classical ballet codified in Carlo Blasis' *Elementary Treatise Upon the Theory and Practice of the Art of Dancing*	1820	
New, unusual gas-lighting effects highlight production of *Aladdin, or the Magic Lamp*	1822	
	1824	First trade union formed in England
Moscow Ballet, now known as the Bolshoi, founded	1825	Aleksandr Pushkin's historical tragedy *Boris Godunov* completed
Debut of Marie Taglioni in Meyerbeer's *Robert le Diable* at Paris Opéra	1831	Victor Hugo writes *Notre Dame de Paris*
Filippo Taglioni choreographs *La Sylphide*, a two-act ballet that stars his daughter, Marie Taglioni; four years later Danish choreographer August Bournonville restages *La Sylphide* to display the talents of Lucile Grahn	1832	
Fanny Elssler causes a sensation in Paris by performing the "Cachucha" during Jean Coralli's *Le Diable Boiteux*	1836	
Noted ballet instructor Carlo Blasis becomes director of the Royal Academy of Dance at La Scala, Milan	1837	Accession of Queen Victoria of England
First production of the quintessential Romantic ballet, *Giselle*, is highlighted by the success of Carlotta Grisi	1841	
Premiere performance of Jules Perrot's *La Esmeralda;* a year later he choreographs the famous *Pas de Quatre* featuring the leading ballerinas of the day: Taglioni, Grisi, Cerrito, and Grahn	1844	Samuel Morse transmits first message over telegraph from Washington, D.C. to Baltimore, Maryland
	1848	Revolutionary movements erupt and are quelled in Germany, Italy, and Austria; Marx and Engels publish *The Communist Manifesto*
Production in St. Petersburg of *The Daughter of Pharaoh*, first successful ballet choreographed by Marius Petipa; seven years later Petipa is appointed director of the Imperial Russian Ballet School, succeeding Saint-Léon	1862	
	1863	Battle of Gettysburg, turning point of the American Civil War; President Lincoln issues the Emancipation Proclamation
Saint-Léon choreographs *Coppélia*	1870	Outbreak of the Franco-Prussian War; a year later France capitulates
Sergei Diaghilev born	1872	
	1874	First major exhibit of Impressionist paintings held in Paris

Italian producer and choreographer Luigi Manzotti stages *Excelsior*, a ballet extravaganza celebrating the triumph of technology

1881

Premiere of Petipa's opulent production of *The Sleeping Beauty*, with music by Tchaikovsky; Loie Fuller creates her signature piece, *The Serpentine Dance*

1890 — First production of Ibsen's character study, *Hedda Gabler*

The Nutcracker, choreographed by Ivanov to Petipa's specifications, poorly received at first performance in St. Petersburg

1892

1893 — Tchaikovsky dies a few days after conducting premiere performance of his Sixth Symphony

Martha Graham born

1894

Ivanov's and Petipa's *Swan Lake* presented in St. Petersburg

1895 — Publication of Freud's *Studies on Hysteria* marks the beginning of psychoanalysis

Isadora Duncan opens her first school of dancing for children in Germany; George Balanchine and Frederick Ashton born

1904 — Moscow Art Theater produces Chekhov's final play, *The Cherry Orchard*

First performance by Anna Pavlova of her legendary solo, *The Dying Swan* in St. Petersburg

1905

Ruth St. Denis scores personal success in performance of *Radha*; four years later she presents her first evening-long dance drama, *Egypta*

1906

First season in Paris for Sergei Diaghilev's Ballets Russes; Diaghilev company presents Michel Fokine's *Les Sylphides*, an early abstract ballet; Isadora Duncan completes the first of four American tours during her career.

1909

Death of Marius Petipa

1910

Vaslav Nijinsky stages his controversial version of *Afternoon of a Faun*

1912

Rioting follows premiere of Igor Stravinsky's *Le Sacre du Printemps*, choreographed by Nijinsky

1913 — First volume of Marcel Proust's *Remembrance of Things Past* is published

Ted Shawn joins the Ruth St. Denis company; they marry; a year later they open the Denishawn School of Dance in Los Angeles

1914 — Outbreak of World War I; Panama Canal opens

Diaghilev's Ballets Russes presents Léonide Massine's *Parade*, with scenery by Picasso and music by Satie; two years later Massine choreographs *The Three-Cornered Hat*

1917 — Bolshevik Revolution deposes tsar in Russia

1919 — Treaty of Versailles ends World War I

Sergei Diaghilev dies in Venice and the Ballets Russes disbands; Serge Lifar appointed director of the Paris Opéra Ballet a year later

1929 — Stock market crash in United States leads to worldwide economic depression

Final performance of Denishawn Company at Lewisohn Stadium Concerts in New York City; the following year Ted Shawn organizes a touring company, Ted Shawn Male Dancers; premieres of two major modern dance works, Martha Graham's *Primitive Mysteries* and Doris Humphrey's *The Shakers*; founding of Vic-Wells and Ballet Club (later Ballet Rambert) in England

1931 — Japanese occupy Manchuria

German choreographer Kurt Jooss introduces his antiwar ballet, *The Green Table*, at an international competition in Paris

1932

George Balanchine and Lincoln Kirstein open School of American Ballet in New York City

1934 — Red Army in China, led by Mao Tse-tung, begins legendary Long March that culminates one year later in establishment of a headquarters at Yenan

Premiere of *Serenade*, first ballet choreographed by Balanchine for the American Ballet, a precursor of the New York City Ballet

1935

Antony Tudor's *Jardin aux Lilas* premieres at Ballet Club in London

1936 — Beginning of Spanish Civil War; three years later forces led by General Franco emerge victorious

Lucia Chase and Richard Pleasant organize Ballet Theatre, known today as the American Ballet Theatre

1939 — German invasion of Poland begins World War II

Ted Shawn becomes director of Jacob's Pillow Dance Festival and University of the Dance at Lee, Massachusetts

1941 — Japanese attack on Pearl Harbor brings United States into World War II

Agnes de Mille choreographs *Rodeo* to a score by Aaron Copland for Ballet Russe de Monte Carlo	1942	
Debut of Martha Graham's *Appalachian Spring*, with music by Aaron Copland; Jerome Robbins and Leonard Bernstein provide choreography and music for Ballet Caravan's *Fancy Free*	1944	Allied invasion of Europe begins; a year later Hitler is defeated
American Ballet Theatre is first postwar American company to tour England	1946	United Nations General Assembly holds first sessions in London; Trygve Lie of Norway is elected first secretary-general
Balanchine and Kirstein's Ballet Society invited to become resident ballet company at New York's City Center for Drama and Music; the company is renamed New York City Ballet	1948	
First Sadler's Wells (Royal Ballet) tour of U.S.; José Limón stages *The Moor's Pavane*	1949	Victory of Red Army in China; People's Republic of China proclaimed
Death of Nijinsky	1950	
Merce Cunningham's *Collage*, first presentation of *musique concrète* in the United States	1952	Gamal Abdel Nasser leads army coup to overthrow Egyptian monarchy
Robert Joffrey founds Joffrey Ballet; Sadler's Wells Ballet renamed the Royal Ballet upon presentation of royal charter; Bolshoi Theatre Ballet's appearance in London marks company's first performances in the West	1956	Suez Canal crisis; Russia crushes uprising in Hungary
Balanchine choreographs one of his most celebrated works, *Agon*	1957	*Sputnik I* launched by the Soviet Union
Premiere of Martha Graham's full-evening dance drama, *Clytemnestra*	1958	Charles de Gaulle elected French president; founding of the Fifth Republic
Black dancer and choreographer Alvin Ailey creates *Revelations*, a dance set to spirituals and folk songs	1960	
John Cranko named director of the Stuttgart Ballet; Kirov Ballet makes first tour through Europe; Rudolph Nureyev defects; a year later Nureyev makes his premiere appearance with Margot Fonteyn at Royal Ballet gala in London	1961	Soviet astronaut Yuri Gagarin becomes first man sent into space; Berlin Wall built
	1963	President John F. Kennedy is assassinated
New York City Ballet's permanent home, the New York State Theater, completed; Ninette de Valois retires as director of the Royal Ballet and is replaced by the company's leading choreographer, Sir Frederick Ashton; six years later Kenneth MacMillan succeeds Ashton	1964	China becomes the fourth nation to explode an atomic bomb
Danish dancer and choreographer Flemming Flindt appointed director of the Royal Danish Ballet	1966	
Premiere of Robert Joffrey's multi-media ballet, *Astarte*	1967	Arab-Israeli Six-Day War
American Ballet Theatre named resident company at John F. Kennedy Center for the Performing Arts in Washington, D.C.	1968	Russian troops invade Czechoslovakia to stifle liberal regime of Alexander Dubcek
Stuttgart Ballet's successful engagement in New York City underscores its development as a leading international company	1969	American astronauts are first men to walk on the moon
Maurice Béjart choreographs his ambitious full-length ballet, *Nijinsky*	1971	
New York City Ballet's week-long Stravinsky Festival honors the composer's contribution to ballet	1972	
Modern dancer and choreographer Twyla Tharp stages *Deuce Coupe* for the City Center Joffrey Ballet; Anthony Tudor named associate director of A.B.T.	1973	Agreement signed to end the Vietnam War; renewed fighting in the Middle East
American choreographer Glen Tetley named director of the Stuttgart Ballet, succeeding the late John Cranko; Harkness Theater opens in New York City; Valery Panov and his wife permitted to emigrate to Israel	1974	Watergate scandal precipitates governmental crisis in United States

Acknowledgments

The author wishes to thank the staff of the Dance Collection of the New York Public Library for assisting him in his research for this book. Invaluable assistance was also provided by Mary Clarke, Selma Jeanne Cohen, George Dorris, Gage and Richard Englund, Henley Haslam, and Walter Terry.

Picture Credits

The following abbreviations are used:

ABT —American Ballet Theatre
BO,P —Bibliothèque de l'Opéra, Paris
BN,P —Bibliothèque Nationale, Paris
CB,M —Civica Raccolta di Stampe Bertarelli, Milan
MS,M—Museo Teatrale alla Scala, Milan

HALF TITLE Symbol by Jay J. Smith Studio FRONTISPIECE (Kenn Duncan)

CHAPTER 1 **6** (Quilici) **8** top, BN,P; bottom, Museo del Bargello, Florence (Bevilacqua) **9** CB,M (Pizzi)

CHAPTER 2 **10** Musée des Beaux-Arts, Rennes (Bulloz) **12** Both: (Pizzi) **13** BN,P (Lalance) **14** BN,P (Lalance) **15** Biblioteca Nazionale, Turin (SEF) **16** Both: CB,M (Saporetti) **17** (AME) **18–19** BN,P (Lalance) **20** BN,P (Lalance) **21** CB,M (Mella) **22** Biblioteca Nazionale, Turin (SEF) **23** Bibliothèque de l'Institut, Paris (Lalance) **24** Both:BN,P (Lalance) **25** BO,P

CHAPTER 3 **26** BO,P (Lalance) **28** BO,P (Pizzi) **29** Musée des Beaux-Arts, Tours (Giraudon) **30** BO,P (Giraudon) **31** Charlottenburg, Berlin (Scala) **32** CB,M (Mella) **33** Bibliothèque de l'Arsenal (Giraudon) **34** BO,P (Giraudon) **35** top, BO,P; bottom, BN,P (Lalance) **36–37** Louvre (Lalance) **38** BO,P **39** BO,P **40** MS,M (Liverani) **41** CB,M

CHAPTER 4 **42** BO,P (Lalance) **44** MS,M (Mella) **45** MS,M (AME) **46** & **47** Both: MS,M (Dani) **48–49** Both: MS,M (Dani) **50** MS,M (Liverani) **51** MS,M (Dani) **52** left, MS,M (Dani); right, BO,P (Lalance) **53** top, BO,P (Mella); bottom, BO,P **54** Musée Carnavalet, Paris (Bulloz) **55** (Ballet West) **56** MS,M (Dani) **57** MS,M (Pizzi) **58–59** Musée du Jeu de Paume, Paris (Scala) **60** & **61** All: MS,M

CHAPTER 5 **62** MS,M (Dani) **64** top, Historical Museum, Moscow (Novosti); bottom, CB,M (Pizzi) **65** State Russian Museum, Leningrad (Novosti) **66** Both: MS,M (Dani) **67** MS,M (Liverani) **68-69** (Picagliani) **69** MS,M (Dani) **70–71** All: MS,M (Dani) **72** top, MS,M (Dani); bottom, *Le Theatre*, May, 1911 **73** *Le Theatre*, May, 1911.

CHAPTER 6 **74** Bibliothèque de l'Arsenal, Paris (Giraudon) **76** Musée des Arts Décoratifs, Paris (Snark) **77** Boris Kochno Collection, Paris **78** Victoria and Albert Museum, London **79** Testa Collection, Rome (Liverani) **80** (Bert) **81** top, Larionov Collection, Paris (Liverani); bottom, Boris Kochno Collection, Paris **82** left (Herbert Migdoll); right, BO,P **83** Boris Kochno Collection, Paris **84** Testa Collection, Rome (Liverani) **85** Musée de la Ville, Paris (Snark) **86** MS,M (Dani) **87** Levante Gallery, Paris (Liverani) **88** Lincoln Center Library **89** top, Boris Kochno Collection, Paris; bottom, Lincoln Center Library **91** Lincoln Center Library **92** Both: Lincoln Center Library **93** Culver Pictures

CHAPTER 7 **94** (Picturepoint) **96** Lincoln Center Library **98** & **99** (San Francisco Ballet) **100** (Martha Swope) **101** Both: (USIS) **102–03** (Martha Swope) **104** (USIS) **105** (Martha Swope) **106** top, Lincoln Center Library; bottom (ABT) **107** (Martha Swope) **108** (ABT) **109** (Kenn Duncan) **110** top (Fred Fehl); bottom (ABT) **111** Both: (Martha Smope) **112–13** (Herbert Migdoll) **114** & **115** Both: (Martha Swope)

CHAPTER 8 **116** (Kenn Duncan) **118** top (Bilderdienst Suddeutscher Verlag); bottom (Zoll) **119** Both: Lincoln Center Library **121** (Ed Wergeles—Newsweek) **122** & **123** Culver Pictures **124** (Costas Cacaroukas) **125** (Zachary Freeman) **126** (Jack Mitchell) **127** (M. Keller) **128–29** (Richard Rutledge) **130** & **131** (Kenn Duncan) **133** (Kenn Duncan) **134** & **135** All: (Fagian)

CHAPTER 9 **136** (International Color Library) **138** (Michael Davis) **139** (International Color Library) **140** (Houston Rogers) **141** AME (Lotti) **142** & **143** Both: (Kenn Duncan) **144** All: (Novosti) **145** (Piccagliani) **146–47** (R. Cohen) **148** (Bernand) **148–49** (Piccagliani) **150** (Dominic) **151** (Ballet West **152** (Photo News Service)

DANCERS AND THE DANCE **154–80** Ten sketches by Edgar Degas. All: Metropolitan Museum of Art, The H. O. Havemeyer Collection, 1929.

Selected Bibliography

Amberg, George. *Ballet: The Emergence of an American Art.* New York: Mentor Books, 1949.

Beaumont, Cyril W. *Complete Book of Ballets.* New York: Grosset & Dunlap, 1938.

Buckle, Richard. *Nijinsky.* New York: Simon & Schuster, 1971.

Chujoy, Anatole. *The New York City Ballet.* New York: Alfred A. Knopf, Inc., 1953.

Chujoy, Anatole and P. W. Manchester, eds. *The Dance Encyclopedia.* New York: Simon & Schuster, 1967.

Clarke, Mary. *Dancers of Mercury: The Story of Ballet Rambert.* London: Adam and Charles Black, 1962.

———. *The Sadler's Wells Ballet: A History and Appreciation.* London: Adam and Charles Black, 1955.

Clarke, Mary and Clement Crisp. *Ballet: An Illustrated History.* New York: Universe Books, Inc., 1973.

Cohen, Selma Jeanne. *Dance as a Theater Art.* New York: Dodd, Mead, 1974.

Cohen, Selma Jeanne, ed. *The Modern Dance: Seven Statements of Belief.* Middletown: Wesleyan University Press, 1966.

De Mille, Agnes. *Dance to the Piper.* Boston: Little, Brown and Company, 1952.

Denby, Edwin. *Dancers, Buildings, and People in the Streets.* New York: Horizon Press, 1965.

———. *Looking at the Dance.* New York: Horizon Press, 1968.

Duncan, Isadora. *My Life.* New York: Universal Publishing and Distributing, 1968.

Fokine, Michel. *Memoirs of a Ballet Master* (trans. by Vitale Fokine, ed. by Anatole Chujoy). Boston: Little, Brown and Company, 1961.

Grigoriev, S. L. *The Diaghilev Ballet 1909-1929* (trans. and ed. by Vera Bowen). Harmondsworth: Penguin Books, 1960.

Guest, Ivor. *Fanny Elssler.* Middletown: Wesleyan University Press, 1970.

———. *The Romantic Ballet in Paris.* Middletown: Wesleyan University Press, 1966.

Karsavina, Tamara. *Theatre Street.* London: Constable and Company Ltd., 1948.

Kerensky, Oleg. *Anna Pavlova*. New York: E. P. Dutton and Co., Inc., 1973.

Kirstein, Lincoln. *Movement and Metaphor: Four Centuries of Ballet*. New York: Praeger Publishers, 1970.

———. *The New York City Ballet*. New York: Alfred A. Knopf, Inc., 1973.

McDonagh, Don. *Martha Graham*. New York: Praeger Publishers, Inc., 1973.

———. *The Rise and Fall and Rise of Modern Dance*. New York: New American Library, 1971.

Migel, Parmenia. *The Ballerinas: From the Court of Louis XIV to Pavlova*. New York: The Macmillan Co., 1972.

Money, Keith. *Fonteyn: The Making of a Legend*. London: Collins, 1973.

Percival, John. *The World of Diaghilev*. New York: E. P. Dutton and Co., Inc., 1971.

St. Denis, Ruth. *An Unfinished Life*. New York: Harper and Brothers, 1939.

Siegel, Marcia B. *At the Vanishing Point*. New York: Saturday Review Press, 1972.

Sorell, Walter. *The Dance Through the Ages*. New York: Grosset & Dunlap, 1967.

Taper, Bernard. *Balanchine*. New York: Harper & Row, 1963.

Terry, Walter. *Miss Ruth*. New York: Dodd, Mead and Company, 1969.

Wigman, Mary. *The Language of Dance* (trans. by Walter Sorell). Middletown: Wesleyan University Press, 1966.

191